LORD, I NEED A HUG

SURVIVING THE TRAUMA OF DIVORCE

Donna Christensen

ACW Press
Phoenix, Arizona 85013

Lord, I Need a Hug

Cover Design by Alpha Advertising, Inc., Sidell IL
Interior design by Pine Hill Graphics

Packaged by ACW Press
5501 N. 7th Ave., #502
Phoenix, Arizona 85013
www.acwpress.com

Library of Congress Cataloging-in-Publication Data

Christensen, Donna.
Lord, I need a hug : surviving the trauma of divorce / Donna Christensen. -- 1st ed.
p. cm.
ISBN: 1-892525-50-X

1. Christensen, Donna. 2. Divorced people--Religious life. 3. Divorce--Religious aspects--Christianity.
I. Title

BV4596.D58C47 2001 248.8'46'092
QBI01-200416

Printed in the United States of America.

Dedicated to...

those whose pillows are wet from the
tears that cannot be counted.

– Acknowledgments –

God has blessed me with three wonderful children: Sharon, Phil, and Stacy. Their words of affirmation and love, followed by phone calls of encouragement, helped me to keep pressing on. I love them deeply.

I thank Joyce Dawes, my sister, best friend, and confidant, for taking full responsibility to care for our mom, an Alzheimer's patient, when I was unable to help. I'm also thankful for my dad's love, concern, and willingness to help me whenever there is a need.

God made a place for me in a Bible Study with Al and Marguarite Stille, Sharon and Preston Stover, Lamar and LaRose Storey, and Jody Ballard. They shared my pain, but also brought great joy and laughter back into my life during the years we met together.

Ken and Carol Van Sickle prayed and kept me accountable in the Word of God. John and Gene Hall, Steve and Kathy Holley, Mike and Martha Lynn Henshaw, and Dottie Britton made room for me on a plane, around their tables, and in their hearts.

Many cups of tea were shared with my special neighbor, Rosie Pierce, while other neighbors kept a watchful eye and helped shovel at least six feet of snow!

Dick and Mary Daum were the "wind behind my back" when I moved to North Carolina. Dick saw merit in my written testimony; Mary read, reread, and kept moving me toward the world of publication.

From Germany, Lee and Diane Lustig continually called, prayed, and encouraged. Our hearts are bound together as we ask God to use this work to encourage others.

To those who are not individually named, know that your deeds of kindness never went unnoticed. I am thankful for all the hugs you gave me from God.

– Contents –

– Foreword –

As a marriage and family therapist, I often encourage my clients to journal their thoughts, feelings, and daily encounters. For those who have experienced significant losses, sometimes this effort produces narratives that lead to new beginnings. This tool allows them to begin framing positive thoughts and plans for their future, as opposed to dwelling on negatives, languishing in depression, or hopelessly entrapped by feelings of victimization.

Donna Christensen, a close family friend, journalized the deep pain and loss she experienced when her husband of thirty years abandoned her. As I began reading her story, I experienced many emotions. Tears of grief flowed freely as she described the pain. Yet as I travelled with her through the written pages of her journey, I experienced joy as I read how she yielded herself to the care of our Lord Jesus Christ, how she looked to Him to meet her deepest need.

Donna's story is one that I knew well. Eight years ago I received a long-distance phone call from her husband. He briefly explained that he was leaving her for another woman. He asked if I would look after her (their oldest daughter is my daughter-in-law). Immediately, my wife and I threw a few things in the car and drove several hours to their home. Donna and her children were experiencing the initial stages of this crisis in their family. After a few days, we went back to our home and responsibilities with heavy hearts. We left behind a lonely, scared, bewildered, and brokenhearted woman whose life had previously been devoted to supporting her husband and rearing their three children in a Christian home. We did not anticipate the work that God was about to do in Donna's life.

As the months and years slipped by, our visits were sporadic, but encouraging. Every time we sat around the dining room table, I was blessed to see how Donna's faith was being strengthened. We enjoyed hearing her laugh as never before, and watched her confidence grow as she began to trust God with her future, no matter what lie ahead. During one of those visits, she graciously shared major portions of her work. I immediately recognized that her story could be an encouragement to thousands who find themselves in similar circumstances. I urged her to have it published as a ministry to others.

I have shared drafts of Donna's journal with clients in my practice and they have all told me how it encouraged them. I recommend this book to Christian counselors, not only as a model of how to journal, but even more importantly, as a way to point their clients to Donna's great God. Hers is a journal that shows us in day-to-day living the path that leads to the only One who can meet our deepest need.

Richard S. Daum, M.A.
Licensed Marriage and Family Therapist

– Prologue –

Please, Come In!

If you came to my home for a visit, I would welcome you at my front door with a big hug! Ushering you down a couple of steps that lead to the sunken family room, we could sit on the over-stuffed sofa I've placed beneath a picture of an English lady tending her garden. It brightens the wall where the family portrait once hung. I would offer you a cup of coffee or iced tea, hoping that you would feel the warmth of this room. As we politely chatted for the first few minutes, I'd point out my latest accomplishment: replacing hum-drum tan curtains with these gardenia-white, tea-rose pink, and heavenly blue window treatments, making this room my favorite.

Knowing that you've come for reasons other than light conversation, I would share a little of where I've been, before my life fell apart.

I fell in love with my high school sweetheart. We both entered college as freshmen, but I ended my studies after my sophomore year. We married during the Thanksgiving break of his junior year. After my husband's graduation with a degree in the field of electrical engineering, our three precious children were born.

Working ten years as an engineer and faithfully serving in the local churches, my husband shared that God had burdened his heart to seek full-time ministry. I agreed to support him in whatever he chose to do, even though *I* felt totally inadequate to be the wife of a minister. But I also didn't want to say to God, "No, You can't have my husband!"

Not long after our decision, the small church we were attending was in need of an associate pastor. The search committee asked my husband to fill this new position. We felt that this was God's affirmation that He had led us to this place.

With our children, ages eight, six, and two, my husband and I said good-bye to our small three-bedroom bungalow and set out on an unknown journey called *ministry.* What an awesome task! With seminary still ahead of us, our home was in constant motion. We juggled our family around breakfast meetings, board meetings, staff meetings, and prayer meetings. From Bible studies to banquets, rehearsal dinners to weddings, and seminary homework squeezed late into the nights, the commitments were endless as the congregation of two hundred steadily grew.

Within ten years, annual Christmas and Easter pageants, presented by a one-hundred voice choir and orchestra, drew large audiences. Growing ministries for singles, the deaf, and youth were all part of this exciting community. In our eighteenth year, architectural plans for a third building program were underway for the two thousand parishioners who worshiped there.

Unending schedules brought fatigue and frustration. Our lives passed in the night. Yet seeing how the church had impacted the lives of so many made it all seem worthwhile—until one November afternoon when my husband of thirty years was seen in the arms of someone else. A few weeks later he turned his back on everything he believed and loved. My heart was ripped in two. I wanted to die!

Now, as our visit continued and I'd refreshed your drink, I would do most of the talking as I excitedly shared what God has done for me; how I'm learning what He means when He bids, "Call to Me, and I will answer you, and show you great and mighty things which you do not know" (Jeremiah 33:3 NKJV). I would also tell you about all the special things that have happened in this very room since then; how I've literally inhaled the fragrance of beautiful worship music, clinging to the message of each song as it ministered to my heart. I've taken notes as I listened to God's men instruct me in His Word. I've sought Him much like a starving woman looks for bread; as one dying of thirst clutches his throat in search for water; or as that desperate woman in the Bible inched her body along a dusty road reaching out as she cried, "If I may touch His garment, I shall be whole" (Matthew 9:21). I don't even know her name...but Jesus does. He spoke to her just as tenderly as He spoke to me: "Daughter, be of good comfort, your faith has made you whole" (Matthew 9:22 KJV).

Treat this book as though we were sitting together on my couch sipping tea or drinking coffee beneath the picture of the lady tending her garden. Perhaps you're walking through some very difficult times right now, and that is why this book was offered to you. I would like to share how God carefully nurtured and tended to my heart. Even though I don't know your name, nor that of the desperate biblical woman, God knows. No matter how difficult your situation may be right now, I know that He is the only One who can enable you to enjoy life again. My prayer is that you will be encouraged as you read selected portions from my journal, giving evidence that God felt my tug at the hem of His garment.

God wants you to reach out to Him for the comfort and strength you need to press on. Allow Him to fill in the pages of your journal with the "great and mighty things" He is waiting to do for you.

– Chapter One –

I Just Want to Die!

The sun shone brightly through the windows in the family room on that cold brisk January morning. Normally, I drew the curtains open so the rays would warm the room. But this morning there was no warmth. I felt as though I was standing in the midst of a cold and frightening holocaust. Words, like rocks hurled at windows, shattered my world into a million pieces when my husband confirmed what I had found concealed in a brown manila envelope. "I am in love with her and she feels the same way about me."

No words could ever describe the intense pain and shock of those moments. In a heap on the floor, my pleas did not change his mind. I was completely helpless when he walked away.

"God!" I cried, "Help me! I can't bear this! Please, just let me die!"

In shock, I immediately called our three children. Two were married and lived several states away. All three came as quickly as possible. Nervously groping with the phone, I then called the church asking to speak to one of the staff. They had to know. Within minutes, friends and church family converged at my doorstep. My eyes, darkened by shadows of unspeakable pain and utter disbelief, met theirs. After we embraced, we stood in shocked silence, gazing at one another like mourners at a wake.

I couldn't hold back the tears when my children finally arrived. Our hearts broke as we held each other. My son made several attempts to confront his dad—but to no avail. The cars of well-meaning friends lined the street in front of the house. My neighbors thought there had been a tragic death. Days ran into sleepless nights. And when I had to tell my children goodbye, it felt as if salt were being poured into my already mangled wound.

Everyone left. Everyone. I was completely alone for the first time ever in my life. That was a hard place to be. Alone. Completely. I sat motionlessly at my kitchen table, exhausted, numb, and grieving. The second-hand on the kitchen clock punctuated this totally desolate, barren time.

Several praise tapes were conveniently within reach. I picked out one and stuck it into the new tape deck my husband had given me a few months earlier at a surprise birthday party planned by friends. As the music began, I thought about that particular Sunday following my party when this gift had been anxiously anchored under the kitchen cabinet. Why was he so agreeable to install it right away? At the time I thought he did it to please me, even though installing things wasn't his favorite thing to do. But that Sunday he couldn't hook it up fast enough. Then, like a sudden slam, it hit me. He was trying to get everything done before leaving!

New, unsolicited, unholy thoughts brazenly forced their way in as I stared out the window. "Well now, look at what *your* God has allowed. You say you believe in Him? You say you love Him? Look at what believing and loving God has brought you! So here is your reward for all that straight and narrow living. If you had done something *really* bad, then perhaps this would be payback, but you never did anything to deserve this! You say there is a God? If there is, then where was He when all of this was going on? If He is supposed to be so *good,* why didn't He stop this from happening!?"

Slam! Two points!

Over and over, the god of this world kept hitting me with vicious accusations. I failed miserably to return even one.

The tape, proclaiming that God's grace was sufficient, continued to play. I cried inconsolably, stopping only to take a breath. Cynically I asked God, "What does that mean, 'Your grace is sufficient for me'?[1] I've heard that all my life and now look at me! If Your grace is so sufficient, then it *has* to mean that somehow You can pick up the pieces of my broken life and put me back together again!"

An unpremeditated remark venomously rolled out of my mouth. "Look what loving You cost me!"

Like a child caught for saying a bad word, I put my hand over my mouth wishing I had never uttered those words. For God penetrated my numbed heart when He responded, "Look what loving you cost *Me*!"[2] As the song continued to play, I confessed, "I can't pick up my shattered pieces and put them back together, Lord! I can't!"

I was frightfully aware of my powerlessness to do anything. Trying to gain composure, I lifted my head from the kitchen table ready to barter with my heavenly Father.

"If I read my Bible everyday, pray, and trust You, even though that will be hard, will You help me? God, can You give me a reason to want to live? Will I ever have that abundant life You've promised?[3] Will I ever experience joy in my life again? If I do, it will have to come from You. But if Your supernatural power doesn't hold me together and joy doesn't come, then You are *not* real and You have *nothing* to offer me. I will keep a journal as proof. You will have to write the pages. And remember Lord, I can't pretend very well!"

With great precision, God chiseled these promises into my heart of stone. "Donna, My grace is sufficient for you, for My strength is made perfect in your weakness. I hear your cries.[4] I am here with you. I will never leave you nor forsake you.[5] It is from Me that you will draw your strength so that you might live. I've promised that you will have an abundant life, and that kind of life is found only in Me.[6] Donna, I want you to believe Me. I want you to trust Me."[7]

– Chapter Two –

Lord, Thank You for the Rose

The week following that war in the kitchen seemed like an eternity. I struggled to do the simplest chores. On one particular day going to the store seemed an insurmountable task, especially with no appetite. The aftermath left me feeling as though my insides had been mangled, making it difficult to eat.

As I pushed the grocery cart past specialty items that had once been on my list, a queasy feeling started in the pit of my stomach. I had no reason to buy them anymore. Ads for decadent ice creams or pizzas seemed a sickening joke; oatmeal was my staple. This queasiness turned into the fear of being recognized as I made my way through the store. Carefully, I glanced around each corner before starting down the aisle.

"Oh Lord, *please* don't let me run into anyone I know. I've seen the way they look at me. They'll just automatically don an expression of pity. I can't bear to hear another well-intentioned 'Are you doing okay?' or 'I'm praying for you.'"

Relieved that I had made it through the check-out without seeing a familiar face, I pushed the half-filled grocery cart next to the curb and loaded my car with the fruit, cereal, and frozen vegetables. On the way home, I stopped by the local gas station to fill up. While pumping gas, the attendant's friend pulled in behind me. After they chatted for a couple of minutes, I overheard, "Do you have any left?"

The friend replied, "A few."

"Well, give this lady one."

So his friend walked to his car and handed me a beautiful long-stemmed rose. My eyes brimmed with tears as I thanked him and got back into my car. More lovely than what I could have imagined coming out of the back seat of an old beat up car, I admired the beauty of this perfectly shaped magenta rose. Its fragrance was an added surprise. As I turned the key, an unshakable thought occurred. *This isn't a coincidence. This is from God!*

"Lord, is this *really* from You?" I asked aloud. "Is this how You're going to let me know You are real?"

In the few moments it took to reach my driveway, God gently affirmed in my heart. "Yes, Donna, this rose is from Me. It's a small expression of My love for you. I want you to know that I'm going to take care of you. Let Me be your Husband now."[8]

Later in the day I had second thoughts. "Was that rose truly from God, or did I just want it to be? Did God really speak to my heart about being my Husband, or did I make it up? Would God do more things like this, or was I so desperate that I'd believe anything?"

Getting ready for bed, I propped pillows behind my back and picked up my journal from the floor. Gazing at the rose on my night stand, I decided to believe that God had given it to me. The ink flowed as I recounted how God had presented it. My last line, "Thank You for this special touch in my life today, Lord. Thank you for the rose," brought a welcomed and peaceful sleep that night.

"How precious also are Your thoughts to me, O God! How great is the sum of them! If I should count them, they would be more than the sand. When I awake, I am still with You" (Psalm 139:17, 18 NKJV).

– Chapter Three –

I Remember Psalm 18

I've *got* to sleep," I admonished myself during the middle of another sleepless night. "I can't depend on sleeping pills!" Staring at the ceiling, I knew I would have to come to grips with my husband's opinion of me. Trash! Someone he crumbled up and threw away.

While restlessly tossing from one side of the bed to the other I asked myself, "What did I do that was so wrong? Was I too boring? Too predictable? Should I have planned exciting get-aways? What if I had been smarter…discussed current books? Would he have respected me more?"

Unable to get comfortable, I plumped up my pillow that had dried from last night's tears. Still more abrasive questions rubbed my emotions raw. Did he resent that I kept to a budget? Was I too cautious? He had been my life! I sacrificed everything for him, even my "rights" to have more time with him. He kept such a busy schedule. Ministry demanded so much time, and I had been understanding. Were those the reasons, or were there others? If there were, he never told me.

From the depths of my heart I knew I had never purposely set out to dishonor or discredit my husband. I had no hidden agenda to destroy our marriage. A trail of deceitfulness had never been present before in our relationship. I had truly loved and cherished my husband and I honestly believed that he had once loved me. Yet I had no answers.

Succumbing to this sleepless night, I reached for the lamp beside my bed. Its light shone on my open Bible. It seemed as though a thousand nights had passed since I had picked it up. A bookmark had been left in the book of Psalms. Immediately my eyes were drawn to these highlighted verses.

> For I have kept the ways of the Lord,
> And I have not wickedly departed from my God.
> For all His ordinances were before me,
> And I did not put away His statutes from me.
> I was also blameless with Him,
> And I kept myself from my iniquity.
> Therefore the Lord has recompensed me according to my righteousness, According to the cleanness of my hands in His eyes (Psalm 18:21-24 NASB).

It was hard to read because tears kept blurring the words. But they were like a soothing ointment that brought relief from those searing questions.

"Lord," I whispered, "Thank You for telling me that *You* know that I didn't wickedly depart from You. I didn't purposely set out to do something so wrong as to cause my marriage to fail. And like the psalmist, 'I did not put away Your statutes from me.'"

My heart melted as I read, "I was also blameless with Him." In those sacred moments God told me, through His written Word, that He saw me as blameless...above reproach. With gratitude I lingered, grasping the thought that this was how God felt about me.

And the next verse, "Therefore the Lord has recompensed me according to my righteousness; according to the cleanness of my hands in His eyes..."

"Oh Lord, of all the verses I could have randomly selected tonight, this is what You wanted me to know. Thank You for seeing me as having clean hands in Your eyes. Even if no one else will ever know, thank You for telling me that *You* know. No matter what I may have done, whether or not I am to blame, tonight I ask You to forgive me."

With my finger I touched every word as I read them over and over again. I underlined those highlighted verses and wrote them in my journal, knowing that I would need to revisit this page many, many times.

– Chapter Four –

Joy Comes in the Morning

Joy! Would I ever experience it again? When the psalmist penned Psalm 30:5, "Weeping may last for the night…" I wondered, what circumstances gave birth to his song? How long did he weep before he could write the next line? As I lay motionlessly on my side of a partially undisturbed bed, I wondered if a flow of tears continually fell as he slept under the stars. And during his night of weeping, were his steps as lethargic and methodical as mine when I descended the stairs to make the morning coffee and listen to tapes I'd heard the night before? Music must have soothed his spirit as it did mine. Far better than listening to the morning news, it helped fill the deafening quietness.

There was no one to say "good morning." No one offered to pour my coffee. No one sent me off with "have a nice day," nor cared whether or not I did. I guess the psalmist had no one either.

And the next line, "…But a shout of joy comes in the morning." Did the psalmist place more emphasis on *shouting,* or was *joy* accentuated? Did he sense a feeling of complete delight, a gladness of heart, or pure exaltation? If so, then without question it must have been supernaturally from God!

On this cold February morning, I cradled my coffee cup to warm my hands while looking at the few pansies that have defied this winter's freeze. They've already survived two ice storms and deep snow, yet their colorful faces turned toward me as if to present themselves as a small bouquet. I wanted so much to believe that God had kept those pansies just for me. First a rose and now this bouquet of winter pansies.

"Is this You, God? Is this another small way to let me know You care? I appreciate it, but I can't help but ask why do You do something so small as to present me with flowers instead of doing something BIG like changing my husband's heart and bringing him back home?"

Still, I listened as Steve Green sang how God can make kings out of shepherds in the "Hidden Valleys" because He is "God and God Alone," while Damaris Carbaugh promised that I was "Never Alone." Choking back the tears, I softly sang the more familiar songs that followed, but with no confidence that what I heard could change my wounded heart.

There was no praise, no joy, only weeping. Perhaps one day there will be joy, but not today.

> Weeping may last for the night, But a shout of joy comes in the morning (Psalm 30:5b NASB).

– Chapter Five –

Valentine's Day

Valentine's Day. The tears wouldn't stop rolling down my cheeks this morning. No amount of make-up could stop the tears nor hide the redness around my eyes.

"Everyone I know has *someone*, God! It's so hard to face this day. There will be no card, no rose, nothing special for me. Jesus, You must have endured days like this. As You loved others, no one understood Your heart either, and not many responded to Your love."

I gave up trying to hide behind cosmetics. I walked out of the bathroom, cupped my hands over one of the four posters at the end of my bed, and I gazed at Katherine Brown's pencil sketch of Jesus holding a lamb. I wondered how the lamb must have felt when Jesus held him. I took a deep breath, closed my eyes, and believed that I was the lamb. With His head near mine, I could almost hear Him whisper…

"I know."[9]

"I care."[10]

"I'm here."[11]

If I were the lamb, perhaps Jesus would gently stroke my head and assure me of His love. "Look at Me, Donna. Don't you know that I love you? I think about you all the time.[12] Allow Me to tell you how very, very special you are, how deeply My love is felt for you. If you'll listen, I'll tell you the story again of how I saw you,[13] I chose you,[14] and I pursued you[15] because I LOVE YOU![16]

"I don't want you to ever grow weary of hearing My love story. If you were with someone special, you would crave quiet intimate moments like this. You wouldn't want anything or anyone to interrupt. Perhaps music would fill the room as you shared your innermost feelings with that special someone. Why can't *we* have such moments? Donna, let *Me* be that special *Someone* in your life!"

Then the Lord reminded me, "Remember, I have loved you with an everlasting love,[17] this Valentine's day and everyday. I will never abandon you—today, tomorrow, or the next.[18] I will always remain faithful to you."[19]

I tucked away these precious promises and headed for work. Jim, one of the five attorneys in the office, bounded through the front door. His steps were always heavy but buoyant. Everyone knew when Jim arrived! This morning I overheard him say to the receptionist, "Here, Kristin, these are for you." He stopped by Judy's office and said, "Here you go, Judy!" From where he was standing, I saw roses cradled in his arms. My station was next. "Here's a couple of roses for you, Donna." Station by station he handed out all the roses as he headed toward his office.

It was everything I could do to contain the tears. I couldn't believe it! The first thing that popped in my mind was my time with God earlier:

"I know."

"I care."

"I'm here."

From the time I was on my knees to the time I got to work, God had somehow orchestrated an incredible plan. Jim was prompted to stop by a store and purchase a dozen red roses. No, this couldn't be just another coincidence. It couldn't. Even the buzz around the office was that Jim had *never* done anything like that before.

"Oh God! Thank you for not forgetting me!" I whispered as I filled the flower vase with water. "Jim doesn't know it, but *You* had him bring me roses! I *do* have Someone who cares! I have You!"

– Chapter Six –

You Have Already Won!

I had first contacted an attorney for advice six months ago. Now he was calling to alert me that my petition for financial support had been filed in the circuit court.

Mounds of paperwork were necessary to defend my reasons for requesting support. For months I felt as though I was hacking my way through a dark and impenetrable jungle. False innuendoes and relentless questions had to be addressed. And lists. A list of living expenses was required to substantiate my needs. A list of projected annual expenses had to be explained. The value of my life had been reduced to cold incalculable lists! I felt exposed to public scrutiny. A total stranger would look for the slightest misrepresentation to challenge or deny. Every penny was subject to rebuttal. No question was overlooked. Nothing was sacred anymore.

I was trying to rely upon God's Word to prepare me for this battle. In the Old Testament book of Judges, chapter seven, God taught Gideon to trust Him when the odds were against him. God requested Gideon to go to the edge of the enemy's camp. There he would hear what was rumored among the troops on the other side. Then God added, "…if you are afraid to go down, go with Purah, your servant, down to the camp."

I was relieved when I read in verse eleven, "…so he went with Purah, his servant, down to the camp!"

God encouraged me with this Scripture about Gideon because I, too, was afraid. I was afraid to appear in court, afraid for what would happen there. Would I win? Would my needs be met? I worried about the person who was to sit in judgment. After all, this was just another domestic case. Having heard thousands already, would he be indifferent or insensitive to my needs at the hearing?

I set aside the Saturday before Friday's court date to pray. In my heart I wanted to be so close to God, so completely immersed in His love and strength, that I wouldn't feel this sharp pain of worthlessness. Sometimes it hurts to live. This was one of those times. I had to fight the one I loved for monetary support.

"Lord, I'm struggling. You tell me that You are *good*, that Your mercies are everlasting and your truth endures to all generations.[20] You say that You will not withhold any *good* thing.[21] I just don't understand. Is going to court *good*? Lord, this is so hard! Am I one whose heart You looked at and said, 'She will not turn back'? Did You say from heaven that I will stand, therefore You gave me a heavier load?

"Lord, I do want to stand, but these last few months have been exhausting and emotionally trying! This furnace is so hot! Am I refined enough, Lord? Have I passed the test? Do You see Your face reflected in me yet?

"From *The Pursuit of God*, A. W. Tozer said dying is not easy. I want to die to all my rights, Lord, but I'm not sure I can. And now I go to court because I am no longer wanted. My value has been bartered between attorneys. I feel as though I am nothing but an unwanted monetary expense. I am treated as cheap merchandise in the eyes of the one who once considered me priceless. I'm not counted worthy by the one who once loved me."

Before the court date my counselor had advised, "Don't think that a monetary award of the court is the deciding factor as to whether you win or lose. A secular judicial system may or may not be fair. If it is not, then God will provide for you in other ways. The one who seeks the Lord is the one who wins the battle. *Donna, you have already won*!"[22]

My legs were shaking as I walked toward the courthouse. I ran my finger down the alphabetical list of approximately forty names in the enclosed glass docket. Latecomers frantically scurried in front of the roster, not wanting to be late for their hearing. "Look at all those names," I thought. "Think of all the broken lives represented by this list alone! And there will be another list on Monday!"

My attorney and I waited by the door with the others who had cases to be heard. When the clerk opened the double doors, I thought about the double doors that opened when I walked down the aisle on my wedding day. *Never* had I believed that I would walk through these doors!

"Lord, thirty years ago my husband and I declared our love for You and each other. We vowed that we would honor and cherish one another, not abandoned and neglect the other. And now, Lord, here we are for all the world to see. We, who are one in Your eyes, who are called by Your name, are now a public mockery of Your greatness! I can't make my husband keep his covenant to me. Lord, this is *not* what I wanted! I can't change his heart! Please protect me as I enter this battlefield. There's more at stake than I can comprehend."

I prayed silently, "*God, are You here*?" wondering whether my question rebounded off judicial walls or was heard by my Father's attentive ear.

The time for my hearing was scheduled last, therefore no one else was in the courtroom when we were called. God was there![23]

"*God, are You here*?" I prayed again. The time allowed before a judge in such a case was no more than thirty minutes.

The judge sat on the bench for an hour and ten minutes. God was there!

"*God, are You here*?" I still questioned.

"Better start praying," my attorney advised, knowing how this judge typically ruled. "She is known to be indecisive. We might not get a judgment on this matter for weeks."

But as soon as the arguments were heard, the gavel fell. No waiting. No deliberations. Judgment was made on my behalf. Support was granted. My requested needs would be met. I wouldn't have to move from our house. I could stay close to friends who encouraged me and prayed for me. God was there! Indeed!

Even though fatigued, I couldn't go to bed until I penned in my journal:

> "Now the same night it came about that the Lord said to *Donna*, just as He had said to Gideon, 'Arise, go down against the camp, for I have given it into your hands. But if you are afraid to go down, go with your servant (attorney), down to the camp, and you will hear what they say; *and afterward your hands will be strengthened* that you may go down against the camp.' So she went down with her servant (attorney). And it came about when Donna heard the account, she bowed in worship."

– Chapter Seven –

Cars, Floor Mats, and God

I needed to buy a car. Though I'd participated in the selection of cars before, I had never actually purchased one alone. I worried about haggling over prices because of a terrible experience my husband and I had had a few years earlier. A flood of relief rushed over me when my friend Gary came to mind. He was my hairdresser's husband who had been in the car business for years. I decided to ask him to go with me.

"Yes," Gary agreed, "I'd be happy to. As a matter of fact, I know a guy who sells Hondas. He'll be fair." So we decided on a time to meet at the dealership the next Friday.

"Lord, You know I don't have a clue about buying a car," I confessed while backing out of the driveway on my way to meet Gary. "I've heard the stories about salesmen who gouge prices and pressure you into buying. Please protect me. Give me wisdom to do the right thing."

After a quick introduction, Gary's friend told me about the special sale going on. "All the cars you'll see today are new; but they are last year's model. The new cars will be delivered in a few days, so we have to move these out as quickly as possible. Let's take one out to see what you think."

I got behind the wheel and we pulled out of the lot. After several minutes into the test drive, I was momentarily taken off guard when the salesman, with genuine sincerity, said, "Gary told me a little about your situation. I want to help you as much as possible."

Instantly, my concern about being ripped off completely vanished. Then, totally out of the blue, I blurted out to this perfect stranger my deep concern for my husband. "He is emotionally in trouble," I insisted. "I know he's made a terribly dreadful mistake, but I've been begging God to bring him back home! I wish he knew my heart! I wish he knew that I would do anything to help him!"

"I'm so sorry," he responded sympathetically.

Thankful for any diversion, at his suggestion I checked out the new bells and whistles as we headed back to the lot.

"What got into me back there?" I was embarrassed just thinking about it!

I looked at a couple other cars with a few more frills along with a higher price tag, but settled on the mint green car I'd driven. With that, the negotiations started. Because the color was new that year, the dealer knocked off a few dollars. He also deducted the maximum trade-in allowance for the old station wagon I was driving. The paperwork was completed in a relatively short time and I was handed a new set of keys. The only glitch was the floor mats. They were out of stock and had to be ordered. The salesman asked if I could stop by next week to pick them up. That worked out well, because I would pass right by there after I picked up my sister at the airport on the way to my dad's house.

Thankful that this ordeal was over, I thanked God for Gary and his friend as I caught a glimpse of them in the rear view mirror waving goodbye.

"Lord, thank You for preparing the way and sending someone who was honest and nice."

Later that evening, I called Gary to thank him for his help. "No problem! By the way, I wanted to let you know that by making your sale, our friend won the bonus for the month! It really helped him."

"How neat! Maybe God blessed him for being so kind to me!" I replied.

"There's something else that might interest you," Gary added. "After you drove away, my friend confessed that he had messed up his life *big time* by getting involved with another woman. He said that he needed to call his wife. I don't know what you said, but whatever it was certainly made an impact!"

Astounded, I put the receiver down as we ended our conversation and backed up against the wall. "Lord, *that's* why I was so bold! *You* put those words in my mouth!"

When Saturday morning rolled around, I hurriedly picked up my sister at the airport. We exited the interstate and pulled into the dealership to pick up the mats.

The receptionist informed me that my salesman was on the lot with another customer. "I'll page him, Ms. Christensen. You can wait in his office."

As I walked toward his cubicle, another woman was sitting in a chair next to his desk.

"I'm sorry," I said, "I didn't know anyone was here."

"Mrs. Christensen?" I heard faintly. "Is your name Donna?"

"Yes."

Then the tears.

Could this be his wife? I wondered silently.

"I just want to thank you for what you shared with my husband last week. I'm here to have lunch with him for the first time in two months. We're trying to put back the pieces."

With that we both embraced and cried unashamedly, knowing the pain we shared.

Cars and floor mats! Who would have thought God would have used floor mats to give me a glimpse of His omniscience!

"God, only You could have planned this!"

"Joy," I exclaimed to my sister as we drove out, "you're not going to believe this!"

My sister was a captive audience to the whole story for the next few hours!

> "But we have this treasure in earthen vessels, that the excellence of the power may be of God and not of us" (II Corinthians 4:7 NKJV).

– Chapter Eight –

What Does It Mean to Be Real?

A wedding invitation from a good friend was so appreciated. I clung to the smallest semblance of social acceptance. It felt good to be invited, to be treated normally rather than pitied. As I stood in the midst of the crowded reception, mingling among friends and acquaintances, I kept bumping into rhetorical questions conditioned for mechanical, uncomplicated responses. Socially correct answers rolled out like cubes from an ice tray; similar, but cold and impersonal.

"How are you doing?" I was asked by an acquaintance.

"I'm doing okay right now, hanging in there only because God is giving me the strength to do so. Thank you so much for asking." With that followed a quizzical look, a polite nod, then a gracious backing away with no reply. All of a sudden I felt conspicuous and embarrassed, wishing that I hadn't been asked.

"Why is it so hard to share with others?" I asked myself while aimlessly wandering among the guests, "Is there anyone who isn't afraid to be *real*—to rip off his mask? What does it mean to be *real*?"

Still tossing around that same question during my Monday morning commute, I had uninterrupted time to sift for answers, that is until a bright unexpected sunrise temporarily blinded me, abruptly interrupting my train of thought. Within seconds, I pulled down the visor, stretching my neck to keep the sun out of my eyes. How convenient! Perhaps people who don't want to be *real* should walk around with visors. One flip of the wrist and reality can be conveniently blocked out! (Saturday's encounter had stung more than I realized.)

After stopping by the deli for a cup of coffee, I pushed the elevator button to the second floor. Friday's unfinished tasks awaited. The monthly bank statement needed to be reconciled, telephone messages demanded a response, and several copying requests had to be at the printers before noon. Time was of essence as our office geared up for another national conference. Volunteers assisted from time to time, and according to my calendar a volunteer was scheduled to come at ten.

When he arrived, we stood at the doorway to the workroom where several hundred letters lay neatly stacked on the table needing to be stuffed and postmarked. Slightly amused at the task, he chuckled, "Well, it's better than sitting at home waiting for the phone to ring!"

After a couple more amicable exchanges, he shared why he had time on his hands. His former job had been eliminated in a corporate downsizing and he was waiting for responses from over two hundred resumes. I asked how he was coping during this difficult time. Surprisingly, he responded with more than the usual "just fine" rhetoric.

"I've struggled with losing my self-worth," he stated openly. "I've had to fight negative thoughts constantly like, 'Why don't you run your car off this bridge;' or, 'You're never going to find a job with the seniority and pay you once had. You're too old now and the job market has passed you by.'"

I concurred, "I know those battles. But they're all lies!"

I probed a little more. "Has anyone been helping or encouraging you?"

"No," he answered. "In the fifteen months I've been unemployed, only three people have called or extended a friendly handshake." He quickly defended the reasons why. "I've told only a few people. It's too uncomfortable for me to admit that I have a need." Then he voluntarily added, "I'm a typical man. I tend to hide my feelings. You know the John Wayne mentality," he continued, "*real* men don't cry!"

Still curious about this significant loss, I asked, "How is your wife handling all of this? Does she have friends who encourage or pray with her?"

"Not really. She purposely keeps herself busy. Right now she's taking a couple of classes at the community college which helps to block it out of her mind. We don't discuss it very much because I don't want to let her know how I really feel. It would cause her to worry."

He ended the conversation by picking up the first of many letters as I ran back to pick up a phone page.

On the way home, I couldn't help but think about this morning's conversation. Why *is* it so hard to let friends know you hurt? What kept this man from sharing his pain with others, from wanting to be real?

As soon as I got home, I searched my husband's library for an old children's book once used as a sermon illustration. *The Velveteen Rabbit* was tucked in among books with much deeper theological truths. But this endearing little tale, read to thousands of children while cradled in parent's arms, imparted more than a lighthearted story about Rabbit. The adults who read between the lines discovered that it *costs* to be real. According to old Skin Horse, there's pain when your hair is being loved off. Loose joints and shabbiness are part of the deal.

Is that what it takes to be real? The rub? Do difficult circumstances rub off one's pretentious veneer, exposing the real person? Even though it can be excruciatingly painful and uncomfortable, is this how God brings out inner beauty?

I know God loves me, but there *has* been a lot of pain. I know that my husband's abandonment was not God's *perfect* will, but His permissive will. This didn't take Him by surprise as it did me. But what about the other things that rubbed? My mom's disease, my dad's unexpected surgery, my sister's cancer scare, and my children's pain? Do they help me to become real, exposing my worn-off places? Does each situation make me looser in the joints, so that I will openly and unashamedly tell others about His story through me?

A rub. I scheduled a flight alone to see my first grandchild. Love mixed with pain as I cradled this little miracle in my arms. My dreams for this grandchild and others to come were dashed against a stone! While rocking him to sleep one night, I whispered, "There isn't going to be Grandma *and* Granddad to enjoy you together, precious little one. When you visit, there's only going to be me."

Another rub. My mom had been afflicted by the dreaded Alzheimer's disease. I didn't know how severe it had become until her long-distance call began the unraveling. "I just sold my house!" That might have been okay with some, but I was shocked because she hadn't bought another house! She had no where to go except to move in with me or my sister. Immediately I called her realtor. "It sold within a few days," she confirmed. "Your mom needs to be out of her house by the end of next month!"

"How could she do this *now* with only two months before Stacy's wedding! I don't have time right now to deal with her needs!"

My emotions were running rampant. Deep down I was frightened because her irrational decisions were confirming earlier suspicions. Mom didn't understand, and that added to my frustration. So I had to ask my boss for more time off to simplify her fifteen years of accumulated stuff and oversee her move to be with my sister in Texas. After packing up her belongings, she stayed with me for a few days before I put her on a plane to Houston. The events had been frustrating. I was exhausted.

The wedding frenzy had already begun. A dress form in the living room modeled the wedding gown awaiting more beads. Sharon's maid-of-honor dress lacked a finished hem.

Gifts were stacked in every unused space in the house. Most of the wedding jobs had been delegated and order was in reach until my air conditioner broke down during these remaining hot days of August!

Another rub. No! This can't happen! Not now!

With that I slumped down in one of the kitchen chairs, held my head in my hands, and cried from total exhaustion. I remembered that Stan, one of the staff pastors, had offered to help me with any major problem with appliances.

"Sue and I will be right over," was his heart-warming reply to my call.

He checked out everything. Fortunately, the only thing wrong was the emergency switch. It was in the off position which affected the power. My mom must have turned it off when she was here. I was thankful that it was such a minor thing.

Afterward, I offered them a glass of iced tea as we sat around the kitchen table waiting for the air to cool. Politely they asked how I was doing. It took a full minute to answer because of the lump in my throat. Then I shared how all of the recent happenings had taken their toll. I was emotionally drained. I felt wiped out and pulled in every direction.

They listened. They understood. Then they began to share about God's faithfulness during some of their bleakest moments. Their story began by telling me about Stan's rare environmental illness. The family had to move to a cabin in the mountains and line the walls with aluminum foil. Having sick children and sleeping in their car on cold nights brought total discouragement. One day, at their lowest ebb, friends came bearing much needed gifts. Overwhelmed by such love and generosity, Stan shared how he stood near the edge of the mountain one evening and reflected on a promise God had given him.

> "Yet [Abraham] did not waver through unbelief regarding the promise of God, but was strengthened

> in his faith and gave glory to God, being fully persuaded that God had power to do what he had promised" (Romans 4:20-21 NIV).

"Those three years were very difficult for us," Stan admitted. "As I turned the pages of my Bible with gloved hands through holes in a Plexiglas box, God taught me lessons I've never forgotten. Now we know the meaning of 'what He promised, He will do.' We were encouraged and our faith was strengthened."

We then joined hands and they prayed while a steady stream of tears persisted down my cheeks.

"I believe there is a point," Sue empathized, "When God does not allow it to get any worse. Donna, in my heart, I don't believe God will allow any more."

With that, we hugged each other and they left.

Pulling myself together, I had much to think about. Not one word of regret came from their mouths. Hearing about Stan and Sue's rubbings helped me to keep going. I felt as though I had been picked up one more time, brushed off one more time, and sent on my way again *one more time*, all because of the love and vulnerability my friends shared with me.

So Abraham did not waver in unbelief but was strengthened in his faith. Do I dare put my name there? Do I dare say, Donna did not waver in unbelief, but was strengthened in her faith?

"Lord, I *did* waver! Did I fail the test?"

"No." I just had to believe that God knew I was wavering, but He also knew I needed to be encouraged, so He made sure I was! It was another opportunity for me to see how He worked.

"Thank you for being real," was the first sentence in a note to my friends. "Thanks for not withholding the truly tough times. I needed to hear how God provided for you in your bleakest moments."

They were not embarrassed by their loose joints nor concerned if their shabbiness was exposed. It encouraged me to know that in the midst of all their trials, they looked to God and He provided. And that is what He did for me.

> "So do not throw away your confidence; it will be richly rewarded. *You need to persevere* so that when you have done the will of God, you will receive what He has promised" (Hebrews 10:35, 36 NIV, emphasis added).

I'd rather live in my fractured world that's real than in a world that is not fractured, but is just a game.[24]

– Chapter Nine –

Christmas— A Treasured Memory!

Christmas. A time for families. A time for festivities. A time to remember Christ—no matter what.

All my children and their spouses made a special effort to be with me this first Christmas after the separation. What an exciting gift! It was wonderful to wrap my arms around each one as they came through the door. Our reunion was tearful yet joyful. Each of us was dealing with the obvious empty place.

How exciting to have my first grandson, four-month-old Matthew, swaddled in his infant seat. His birth was such a delightful gift. Between his smiles and cooing, this little bundle brought so much joy into this afflicted home. Clanging dishes, big brother's teasing, laughter, and a small baby's cries were the sweetest music I'd ever heard! We played table games and talked for hours. They tackled every chore. To keep things moving, a Spatula Award was up for grabs. Ballots would be cast at the end of the holiday for this coveted award!

One evening, my new son-in-law asked us to pile into the family room for a "tell-me-what-you-think" presentation. He introduced his new idea: "a bit of Scripture along with a bit of chortling" in the form of humorous Christian greeting cards. One by one he held up his newly designed cards.

"Those from Italy send you their greetings..."
(Hebrews 13:24 NIV).

"...In fact I gave them your calling card number!
Happy Birthday!"

They were all hilarious! Seeing one card after another, we doubled over with laughter!

"He's got it!" we unanimously acclaimed. That night it was official. TON (Thinking Outside the Norm) Communication's *It's In The Bible*™ was born.

Loving every minute of our togetherness, I wanted to create a memory. So one night after dinner, knowing that it would be a long time before we would sit around the table again, I asked if everyone would share a sacrifice of praise. It had to be a sacrifice, for all of us carried our deep hurt inside. As I listened to each one of them, I was sure God's heart had been moved by their expressions of gratitude—as was mine!

Then I asked how we might pray for one another during the coming year. With baby Matthew still asleep in his infant seat, we bowed and prayed for each other. Tears of joy filled my eyes—just like God's, I'm sure.

My son Phil later drew me aside and whispered assuringly, "Mom, what we did tonight around the table—this is who we really are."

I wished I could have taken this scene and wrapped it up in a box with a great big bow—to open it again and again, never forgetting that sacred time. For there is no gift they could have given me that would have satisfied my heart more than the gift of themselves. There was nothing they could have done that would have made my heart love them more than I already did. *I loved them simply because they were mine!*

This must be how it is with God. There is nothing I can do to impress Him.[25] There is no gift I could give Him that would cause Him to love me more than He already does.[26] He loves me simply because I'm His!

Thank You God, for Your gift of love!

– Chapter Ten –

I Need a Place

This morning's frigid temperature was all I needed to start a fire in the fireplace. The heat kept most of the downstairs warm. The logs blazed most of the morning, but were reduced to flickering embers by early afternoon. Plummeting temperatures combined with high winds have set new records during this extraordinary deep freeze. The house creaked as the icicles, the size of stalactites, hung treacherously from the gutters. Anxiously I walked from room to room checking to see if melted ice had seeped through.

As the bright sun reflected on the ice-laden trees across the street, they became a breathtaking picture framed by the partially frosted window in the kitchen. During the last couple of nights these same trees, beautifully silhouetted against the street light, couldn't be any less bold than what Monet or Renoir could have painted. It drew me to take in this spectacular beauty…alone.

"I need a few more logs," I directed my soliloquy to the scraggly poinsettia on the hearth with only a few blooms and limp leaves. I brought in an arm load of wood, careful not to knock over this last remnant of Christmas. During the holiday its blooms had added cheeriness to the room. I didn't have the heart to throw out. These freezing temperatures must have shocked it, too!

Thankfully, the cold snap had waited until after Christmas. The weather dominated most of the news as reporters warned people to stay inside. Wearing my warmest sweat suit, I shivered, not because the house was chilly, but from a cold that could not be measured in degrees. I was alone on New Year's Eve. As the fire crackled, I sat close while leaning my head against the sofa.

"It's so cold...and so quiet," I told this poor unsuspecting plant. Its droopiness confirmed my statement. "I feel like such a misfit! As a matter of fact, I feel like you look! I wish I knew where to fit in," I continued airing my complaints with the only other living thing in the house. "Even my kitchen table offers an open invitation to sit anywhere I choose. When I go to church, it's hard to know which class to attend. Am I a couple, with one part missing? Do I decline invitations when couples mostly come? I've even been labeled "generic" by the post office without my approval.

"Oh, how I long to have my own special place. Not just for tonight, but a place that will never change. A place filled with love. A place that's inviting, warm, and friendly! A place where there is joy—like this past Christmas!"

Heaven.

I wasn't thinking about heaven a couple of seconds ago. I was thinking about this cold and lonely night.

Heaven. When spoken quickly or matter-of-factly, it denoted a celestial place referenced in the Bible.

Heaven. When spoken softly or longingly, stirred up a far deeper meaning than a place. It embraced words like "safe," "home," and "joy."

"God, is *this* You?"

Heaven cost Jesus so much in order that I might call it home. Thoughts of heaven prompted me to leave my warm spot for a small cup of grape juice and a cracker. I returned to the family room and sat a little closer to the fire.

As the cracker dissolved on my tongue, I remembered Jesus' sinless body that hung from a cruel cross. A sip from the cup brought tears as I pictured the agony when His blood poured from His side onto the ground. The Lamb of God, with outstretched arms, made it possible for me to be in heaven one day. He endured the pain so that I could have a place with Him forever.

One day I will hear Jesus say, "Come, Donna, I've prepared a place for you![27] Come, sit at My table."[28]

A *place.*

My place.

I glanced at the cover of a magazine with a beautifully decorated table prepared for holiday guests. I envisioned heaven's long table. Will it be set with exquisite place settings? How will the food be presented...on gold and silver trays? Who will sit next to me? I longed for the fellowship that would continue for eternity.

Heaven.

Home.

One day it *will* be all right! One day I will be at the place my Father has lovingly set for me. One day it will never be cold and lonely again. One day He's coming—for me!

> "[So, Donna,] let not your heart be troubled; believe in God, believe also in Me. In My Father's house are many dwelling places; if it were not so, I would have told you; for I go to prepare a place for you. And if I go and prepare a place for you, I will come again and receive you to Myself; that where I am there you may be also" (John 14:1-3 NASB).

– Chapter Eleven –

Just Hold Me, Lord

I have been legally separated for one year which met the state's requirement before my husband could file for a divorce. I shouldn't have been so shaken when he called to schedule a time to discuss a property settlement agreement, but I was. My world fell apart once more. His words felt like a hot iron branding "Rejected" on my heart. Determined not to break down again at work, I said into the phone, "I'm sorry, but meeting with you will be impossible." His inflamed accusation of running up unnecessary legal bills were the charred remains of our conversation.

Driving home, I hoped the cars next to me wouldn't notice my crying as we waited for a light to turn green. The thought of seeing a petition for a divorce plastered on my front door was horrifying. "Lord," I sobbed, "I'm so embarrassed. I'm so ashamed!"

It was dark when I drove in the driveway. My headlights beamed on the only unlit house in the cul-de-sac. Even though it was still early, I went upstairs to get ready for bed, hoping sleep would take me out of this misery. I pulled the covers down, leaving the other side undisturbed. I lay motionlessly, trying hard not to think about that call. I gazed at Katherine Brown's picture of Jesus holding the lamb. I knew God heard the sobs, the crying out in disbelief, and the call for help. "Lord, I can't pray right now. Just hold me the same way You're holding that lamb. Please help me!"

Bible verses I had once memorized flooded my mind. I didn't want to be bothered, but they refused to budge. In an attempt to appease what I considered annoying interruptions, I picked up my third journal, soon to be filled, and wrote down every verse, fragmented phrase, or dangling word. With the help of my new *Strong's Concordance*, I found each text. When the last line was written, I knew it was special. Those Scripture verses composed a personal letter God sent me during that long and difficult night.

> My dear, dear Donna,
>
> I am here with you.[29] I hear your cries.[30] I want to share what I can do if you'll let Me. I can give peace, not the peace the world gives, but supernatural peace. The peace I give will pass all human comprehension and understanding.[31] But you must trust Me.[32]
>
> I know you hurt. I hurt too,[33] but leave the vengeance to Me.[34] I will repay in the way I see fit. I am a just God[35] and a righteous God.[36] Leave those things to me. Are you listening? Be still and know that I am the great I Am. I am God.[37] I have seen your heart. I know it is stayed on Me. I continually look throughout the earth that I might strongly support those whose hearts are completely Mine.[38] Donna, I see your heart.
>
> I know it is hard for you to understand now, but eventually you will see that I am the giver of every good and perfect gift.[39] I am committed to you. I will never leave you nor forsake you,[40] not

now, not ever. I see your weakness. I know you are tired. And in your weakened condition, trust me with what has happened. I will live out My life in you. Because when you are weak, like you are tonight, I will make you strong![41]

Love,
God

Holding His letter next to my heart, I replied, "Lord, You know that I didn't want this to happen. I've prayed and prayed that the heart of the one I love would change. Why does he continue to turn away from You? Why won't he come back home? God, please help me!"

"Hear my cry, O God!
Give heed to my prayer.
From the end of the earth I call to Thee, when my heart is faint;
Lead me to the rock that is higher than I.
For Thou hast been a refuge for me,
A tower of strength against the enemy.
Let me dwell in Thy tent forever;
Let me take refuge in the shelter of Thy wings" (Psalm 61:1-4 NASB).

– Chapter Twelve –

Come to the Garden Alone

Spring! I wished I could put my arms around it and never have to think beyond warmer weather, budding forsythia and lingering crocuses. What a welcomed relief! I kept in touch with my attorney through the proceedings after my husband filed for a divorce. I also kept in close touch with my heavenly Father. As we walked hand in hand, there were many times I looked to Him in disbelief at what was going on. No matter how eloquently the opposing attorney argued, or how precise the legal jargon, nothing filed or certified could make this right.

With the paperwork nearly completed, one last nail—a Final Decree of Divorce—remained to be hammered into the casket of my marriage. By law, its death was imminent.

So today I needed fresh air. I decided to eat my lunch in the car while driving around town with my windows down. I turned on a local Christian station thinking I would catch the news and listen to music. Instead, a Chinese pastor was introduced. He was going to give his testimony about God's sustaining power during an eighteen-year imprisonment. His penalty was purposely severe, the announcer informed, to make him an example for others who might follow his Christian teaching.

"The communist forces will go to any means to stop the spread of Christianity. Those in positions of power do not want to hear that eternal life with God is only possible through Christ alone. Punishing pastors was one way they tried," explained the guest pastor. "But we know that the gospel of Jesus Christ can never be stopped."

He was assigned to work in a cesspool of human waste — the most humiliating and degrading job within those prison walls. The unbearable stench permeated his skin. During those eighteen years, he worked alone, ate alone, and slept alone.

But each morning, in preparation for the day's work, he *chose* to look at those fields as his garden.

"I sang as loudly as I wanted," he shared, "because no one could stand to be near me, not even the guards!"

He quoted the first verse of one of his favorite hymns, "I Come to the Garden Alone." Having sung it as a child, I whispered along with him.

"After I was released," he said in closing, "Many young pastors sought me out to ask, 'How *did* God sustain you?' Then they added, 'Because *when* this happens to me, I want to stand just like you!'"

With tears brimming, I couldn't shake the intensity of his message. There was no way he could have withstood this alone. In times of deep despair, God must have ministered to him through the Scriptures he knew. His strength to face another day had to have been God's strength! God must have supernaturally kept his hope alive. How *could* he have sung? How could he have even thought about gardens, flowers, even the scent of a rose? How could he have endured the loneliness and faced such humiliation had it not been for God?

"Power!" I exclaimed aloud in the car. "It has to be *Your* power, God!"

I compared my circumstances with his. "Lord, I have Your Word so that I can read it, study, and learn. He had what he'd memorized. I listen to music played by orchestras, sung by professionals. He heard the cries of inmates. I have friends who check on me, send notes of encouragement, and invite me to dinner. He had no visitors. It seemed that even though he had nothing, yet he had *everything*!"

I grasped to understand the miracle that God had performed in this man's heart. In his surrounding stench of evil, God cultivated something much more fragrant and far more spectacular than the most beautiful gardens in the world: bouquets of unbelievable joy and overwhelming praise flourished from the fertile soil of his heart.

I felt exposed, sickly, and deficient, wanting to hide the condition of my heart. My husband's broken promise reeked with the stench of evil, but after hearing this man I was without excuse to believe that I could never rejoice again.

"Lord," I prayed in the parking lot before going back into the office, "Whatever it takes, that's what I want. I know my heart needs a lot of work, so I ask that You pull up the weeds that choke out Your promises. Cultivate the places where my roots are shallow, and pour Your living water to soften the places that have grown hard. In spite of my circumstances, I want to become a delightful fragrance too![42] One day, I want others to say of me, 'I want to stand just like you!'"

> "I pray that the eyes of [my] heart be enlightened so that [I] may know what is the hope of [Your] calling, what are the riches of the glory of [Your] inheritance in [me], and what is the surpassing greatness of [Your] *power* towards [me] who believe[s]" (Ephesians 1:18, 19 NASB, emphasis added).

– Chapter Thirteen –

Lord, I Need a Hug

Today as I was driving home, I sensed that there was something I needed, but couldn't quite define it. I wasn't terribly depressed or overwhelmed. Tears had not ruined my makeup during the day. Puzzled by this feeling, I shrugged my shoulders as I drove home in silence. The closer I got to my driveway, the clearer my thoughts became. "I know what it is! *I need a hug*!" A hug would be a little reminder that I am special to someone, that someone special cares for me.

I opened the kitchen door, deposited my briefcase and purse on the kitchen chair, and bounded for the stairs. Kneeling by my bed, I said, "Lord, you know exactly how I'm feeling. I don't know how You will do it, but I just need a hug from You right now. I need a little reassurance that I am special to You."

I pictured my Father slightly bending His knees with outstretched arms, ready to pick me up and whirl me around. I wanted to feel a big burly hug, one that said, "I've been waiting to do this all day!"

While in my familiar spot on my knees, I opened His Word like a treasure of great wealth thumbing through the passages that told my heart, "I love you, Donna![43] You are so special to Me! Go, now[44]...and remember, I *do* love you!"[45]

How could I describe a message so priceless? Words could not adequately express the those tender moments. All I knew was that after kneeling at that place, I felt loved. No profound theological dissertation, just a tender touch of His love.

"Oh, Lord, thank You for caring about the little things in my life—even my need for a hug."

Every night when I come home from work, God is waiting for that hug, but do I take the time to go upstairs to receive it? Not always. At times I get too preoccupied. My own agenda preempts those special times with Him. Sadly, when I'm too busy, I miss out on all those tender moments and loving touches He wants to share with me. And sometimes a hug is all you need!

> "For He has satisfied the thirsty soul, And the hungry soul He has filled with what is good" (Psalm 107:9 NASB).

– Chapter Fourteen –

I Encourage You

It's exciting to watch a triumphant runner cross the finish line. Sophisticated equipment determines winners in a matter of milliseconds. Friends of the runner who got up in the grueling early morning hours to clock his time, or ran with him when another lap seemed impossible, now celebrate in his victory!

As I run the race[46] that God has for me, I also have friends who were there. Not everyone has the gift of encouragement, but God sent a special friend, Carol, with such a gift. Her packages, wrapped with love and concern, were found in a cheerful phone call, a card in the mail, a time of prayer, or a meal around her table.

In the past, dinner invitations turned into social obligations, but now they are intimate times of fellowship. Carol's invitations were a reminder that she had placed value on my life. When I knocked at Carol's door, she always received me with open arms. Her hug assured me that she was expecting me. Come to think of it, that's how God is!

Carol called early this morning before work. "I've just read the first chapter of II Thessalonians and thought of you. I wanted to share these verses."

As I listened, my heart beat with excitement with the overwhelming thought that God was so incredibly sensitive to have placed *my name* on Carol's heart. I reached for my Bible to follow along:

> "We ought always to give thanks to God for you, brethren, as is only fitting, because your faith is greatly enlarged, and the love of each one of you toward one another grows ever greater; therefore, we ourselves speak proudly of you among the churches of God for your perseverance and faith in the midst of all your persecutions and afflictions which you endure. This is a plain indication of God's righteous judgment so that you may be considered worthy of the kingdom of God, for which indeed you are suffering" (II Thessalonians 1:3-5 NASB).

What an encouragement! God provided me with a friend who was adorned with jewels of a pure heart, a good conscience and a sincere faith.[47] There were times when she ran with me, and other times she faithfully stood by the sidelines cheering me on. She prayed for me, listened to me, and held me accountable for what I was studying in God's Word. That's what friends are for!

"Thank you, God, for friends like Carol!"

> "I have called you friends, for everything that I learned from my Father I have made known to you" (John 15:15b).

– Chapter Fifteen –

It's Okay, Lord

Friday morning the phone rang while I was getting ready for work. Karen and Bruce called to say that they were praying for me. "We hope you've planned something special because it is supposed to be an absolutely beautiful weekend," they cheerfully said before going out of town.

Having been in their home many times, they knew my struggle with the weekends. I was thankful that God had placed me on their heart, prompting them to lovingly reach out, so I politely thanked them for calling and wished them an enjoyable time at the shore.

Slowly I put the receiver down and started putting my make-up on in front of the bathroom mirror. "What can I do?" I asked the mirror. "I don't have any plans! I went to my dad's last weekend, visited Sharon a couple of weeks ago. Lord, I *don't* have a place to go, and no one has called!"

It was hard to put on make-up when mixed with tears. The streaks made road maps down my face. That phone call, even though appreciated, had stirred up panic I had tried so hard to suppress. Once again I found myself standing in the same old intersection between "alone" and "left out." And that feeling in the pit of my stomach started again—that gnawing feeling as if I'm sick, but really not.

The mirror reflected more than my image. It revealed what was welling up inside. "All I have is God this weekend and that's not enough!" Translated more precisely, I meant that if I wasn't invited anywhere or I didn't have somewhere to run, then it would be the pits to have to spend the weekend alone with God.

Stunned at what I had spewed out, I wondered how God felt. Deliberately, I laid my brush down by the sink, walked into my bedroom and fell on my knees.

"Oh God, I'm sorry! I must have hurt You. I was so wrong. If I were You, *I'd* be hurt by my words. Lord, I just want to tell You that it's okay. Please help me to consider this weekend as Your special time You have planned for us. I *will* be thankful that You are here with me. Even though my stomach churns because of the unforeseeable emptiness between now and work on Monday, I *will* thank you for this weekend, no matter what!"

Rushing to the office, I settled down at my desk, hoping no one would notice the extra makeup under my eyes or ask about my weekend plans.

Around two o'clock in the afternoon my friend LaRose, who worked across the street, stopped by. In her customary cheerful manner she asked, "What are you doing for dinner tonight?"

"Nothing much," I answered, believing that if I added the word "much" she wouldn't pick up on how desperately lonely I was feeling. She told me that some mutual friends were coming over for a cook-out and asked if I could join them.

"I'd love to!" I exclaimed. "Thank you so much!"

I was so excited! The palpitations of my heart were loud enough to reach the angels in heaven who could rejoice with me! I was beyond words to describe the joy I was feeling. It wasn't just the invitation, although that was huge, but I *knew,* I *KNEW* that God had done that for me.

"Oh, Lord! Thank You! Thank You! Thank You!" I sang joyfully on my way over.

It was a perfect summer evening with the temperature near seventy and candles flickering in the gentle breeze. I enjoyed a delicious meal cooked on the grill with dear friends under an umbrella of bright stars. We laughed as we listened to the guests' adventures of floating on a barge down the Seine River during a recent missions trip to France. I couldn't remember the last time I had laughed so hard.

As I drove home that night, praises reverberated from the front seat of the car to the back. "I can't believe You did this for me, Lord. I just can't believe it. This is who You are! This is what You do! You are my Father who even cares about my weekend! Thank You so much!"

> "[My] mouth was filled with laughter, [my] tongue with songs of joy...The Lord has done great things for [me]. The Lord has done great things for [me], and [I] am filled with joy" (Psalm 126:2, 3 NIV).

– Chapter Sixteen –

Abba Father

Lord, the news today about my dad hit me so unexpectedly. I feel like Bozo, the inflatable punching bag. Wham! and I'm hit again. Can I ever stand without bobbing? Will there ever be a time when I'm out of range?"

"Emergency surgery" was the long-distance report I received from one of my dad's friends. "Your dad needs corrective surgery because of a blocked intestinal tract that has developed from his cancer surgery ten days ago."

I swallowed hard, knowing that once again I had to face another unknown. With tears over my dad's surgery, I knelt by my open bedroom window looking between the trees towards heaven. I didn't want the leaves to block my view; I needed a direct line. I called His name and I was deeply connected to the One who loves me more than I'll ever know. My heart began to settle down knowing that I was in His presence and could share the fear that was in my heart. I pleaded, "Please don't let there be another loss. Please! I can't bear to lose anyone else, God! I just can't!

"Jesus, it must not be a coincidence that last week I thought about You in the Garden of Gethsemane. On Your knees You cried out in pain to the One who knows You most. You cried out to Your Father. There was no one else who could have met the needs of Your heart. *Abba Father.* Those tender words must have been spoken confidently yet so painfully between the Son and His Father, knowing what was ahead for You. *Abba Father.* The compassionate, loving and understanding heart of the Father heard His Son's cry."

Then God shared with me, "Donna, just because you are my daughter, God has sent forth the Spirit of His Son into *your* heart, crying *Abba Father.*[48]

"Cry to Me!" God said.

"*Abba Father*...Daddy." My cry was only a whisper, lest my voice turn to tears again. "*Abba Father*, please protect my dad."

A telephone solicitor invaded these most intimate moments. Exasperated at the rude interruption, I abruptly hung up and called to my *Abba Father* again.

The neighbor cranked up his mower, the engine rudely backfired into my window. That longing I had, like a child who has been hurt and needing to be comforted, was slipping away.

A continuous battle was being waged between the god of this world and the one who was on her knees. St. Paul wrote, "He is always wrestling in prayer for you, that you may stand firm in all the will of God, mature and fully assured" (Colossians 4:12 NIV). The enemy stalks a praying believer's heart, waiting for opportunities to enter unnoticed.

"Press on!"[49] I was reminded. "Resist the enemy and he will flee.[50] Press on!"

I continued to pray. Persistence allowed me to break through the barrage of noise and enter into the glorious place that is beyond the reach of the enemy. Subtle were the ways of this evil one who desperately tried to discourage me from spending time with my *Abba Father.*

I entered His courts where the angels continually sing praises to God.[51] I came boldly to His throne of grace so that I could receive mercy and find grace to help me in my time of need (see Hebrews 4:16 NIV). There had been times when I entered with praise and thanksgiving, but today I burst in with tears and asked Him to watch over my dad. I could approach His throne because I am His child. I have His name. I belong to Him.

In the hours that followed the second surgery, I sat in the corner of the recovery room. A nurse cupped my dad's hands around a pain button. "When the sharp pains come, just press this button," she instructed.

As the hours passed, he would intermittently be awakened by pain. Groggily, he looked around the room, saw me sitting in the corner, and asked, "Are you still here?"

I responded by getting up and walking over to him. Trying to comfort him, I responded, "Yes, Daddy, I'm still here. Go back to sleep."

I thought how nice it would be if I had a "pain button." Whenever a wave of rejection swept over me, I could just press it and be powerfully inoculated. Even though life doesn't offer such a dose, I needed to practice what my dad had done—to open my eyes and ask, "Father, are you still here?"

His reply will always be, "Yes, Donna, I'm still here. You can rest now."

Watching my dad in his senior years go through that ordeal was so hard. I wished I could have relieved some of his pain from two surgeries in ten days. His recovery time was lengthy but successful. Three weeks were added to his hospital stay. After driving four hundred miles for six consecutive weekends to check on him, there was finally rest.

"Thank You, my Father, for giving me more time with my dad. And thank You, too, for helping me better understand what it means to have You as my *Abba Father.* Thank You for not becoming weary when I continually cry out to You. That's what You want me to do, isn't it, to come to You, the One who knows me intimately? And when I do, You tenderly lift my head[52] with

Your hands and smile as Your thumbs wipe away the tears that fall, assuring me that I am safe in Your hands once again. I am safe because You are my *Abba Father*."

> "But Jesus said, 'Let the children alone and do not hinder them from coming to Me; for the kingdom of heaven belongs to such as these'" (Matthew 19:14 NASB).

– Chapter Seventeen –

Where Is Your Faith?

This morning my counselor asked, "Donna, as you are having more opportunities to respond to those who have seen God's power in your life during these stormy eighteen months, what is it that you want them to know?"

I thought for a few seconds and then answered, "That there is hope *after* the pain."

He responded by asking another question. "Don't you believe that there can be hope *in* the pain?"

"How do you know when you have hope?" I asked, not knowing whether I had clearly understood the question. Our discussion led to the definition of hope.

"There is hope," my counselor advised "When there is clarity in chaos."

After I left his office I searched for passages in the Bible where chaotic situations existed. In the eighth chapter of the book of Luke, Jesus' disciples were caught in a storm at sea. There was definitely chaos! Jesus was asleep in the bottom of the disciples' fishing boat when strong winds blew across the water. I could almost hear the disciples frantically shouting above the winds as they were taking on water.

"Lord, wake up! We are perishing!"

"Master! Master! We are going to drown!"

I focused on the reaction of the disciples. How did they respond when their lives were touched by circumstances over which they had no control? Was there clarity in their chaos? I read to Whom they cried. "*Master*!"

The disciple Matthew described the storm as "furious" and recorded what Jesus asked them in the midst of it all: "You of little faith, why are you so afraid?"[53]

"Lord, You knew the disciples were drenched with fear. You saw how they were frantically holding on as the winds tipped their boat in the deepest part of the sea. You were there! You knew that their boat could have snapped at any time. Humanly speaking, if it had, they would have never made it to shore. And in all of that you asked, 'Where is your faith?'[54]

"If *I* had been one of those disciples and had a few minutes to think about your question, I might have answered, 'Well, Lord, I know about all the great things You have already done. I saw You heal the blind and the lame. I was with You when You fed those thousands of people. I heard about the water being changed to wine. And when You cleansed a man of leprosy, everyone was astonished. You even raised Lazarus and Jairus' daughter from the dead! Lord, those were fantastic miracles! And what joy You brought to those whose lives You touched while all the time proving to a doubting world that You are God! But when You were performing those miracles, *my* feet were firmly planted on solid ground. I could have answered You a lot easier if my boat wasn't being tossed around in this relentless sea! You ask me, 'Where is my faith?'

"Lord, how can you expect an answer when these angry waves hurl my boat as if a toy? The spray stings my face like pellets. The oars are slipping out of my hands as I struggle for control. Salt water stings the open cuts on my hands, washing the blood away as if nothing happened. *This is the reality of my storm*!

"I'm shivering. My blue lips tremble. Darkness multiplies my fear as I bend over to keep the knot in my stomach from cramping up. The sea opens up and roars that I am going to perish. And my boat which I thought was my security is beginning to crack! *This is the reality of my storm!*"

Then the Lord asked me, "Where is your faith, Donna?"

"What did you say, Lord? I can't hear You over this clapping thunder!"

"Where is your faith, Donna? Is it in Me, or in your boat?

"Where is your faith, Donna? Is it in Me, or in your ability to finesse the seas?

"Where is your faith, Donna? Is it in Me?"

In all my struggling, all the toil, all the pain and fear that I've encountered, I had only one answer.

"Lord, I cannot save myself in this ravishing storm!"

He asks again, "Where is your faith?"

"Lord, if You don't intervene, I will surely die."

> "He rebuked the wind and the surging waves, and they stopped, and it became calm" (Luke 8:24 NASB*)*.

I asked, "Lord, couldn't You have prevented the disciples from having to go through that storm?" I knew He'd answer "Yes!"

If He had, then I would have never read what the disciples said afterwards:

> "Who then is this, that He commands even the winds and the water, and they obey Him?" (Luke 8:25 NASB).

"Lord, couldn't You have prevented *my* storm...*my* rejection...*my* pain?"

Again, I was sure He'd say "Yes." But if He had, I never would have known what it has meant to be comforted by the

Holy One. I would have never known that Jesus could care for me as my Husband. I would have never experienced the empowerment by the Spirit of God to proclaim His name openly and excitedly at any given opportunity. Even though surging obstacles have battered my boat, I could never be more secure than knowing that Jesus is there with me.

What do I want people to know about the working of God's power in my struggles?

"Lord, You are all I have. Master, You are all I need! *You* are the clarity in my chaos. You are my hope *in* the pain!"

> "Take courage, it is I; do not be afraid" (Matthew 14:27 NASB).

– Chapter Eighteen –

Sacrifice of Praise

My posture of kneeling before the throne of grace had become comfortable. Knowing how I've prayed, a friend teased, "One of these days you're going to have knees like a camel!"

"That's okay," I laughed as I remembered seeing camels' knees while in the Holy Land several years ago. Our tour bus had stopped at a roadside stand to buy bottled water. Two men with four camels *happened* to be at the same stop. The owners, seeking a few American dollars, cried out, "One dol'la! Just one American dol'la to ride the camels!"

I purposely kept my distance, not only because of the smell, but from those crafty Bedouins! A naïve tourist walked toward them, wanting to have her picture taken on the back of a camel. Unexpectedly, one of those huge, baggy animals, with dirt caked on his callused knees, lowered his head and slurped this hapless woman across the face with his long wet tongue! Everyone laughed hysterically—from a distance!

Daily I was on my knees, no matter their condition. Like a soothing ointment, that time brought healing to my heart and mind. Having experienced more and more of God's intervention in my life, seeing His mighty hand at work, my faith increased. My confidence grew stronger. It wasn't unusual to awaken with a verse or a song. But early this morning, God chose something else.

"Donna, I've heard all of your effectual fervent prayers.[55] I know you intimately—even the number of tears you have cried.[56] Your praise during many difficult days have been like incense throughout the heavens. The angels rejoiced because you have chosen to obey those things you know to do.

"I've listened as You continually asked that your marriage be restored, despite the divorce proceedings. You prayed that your husband would be so miserable that he would change his mind and *want* to come back home. But he hasn't.

"Will you still love Me and seek Me if what I give you is not what you have asked? Will you trust My master plan even if it doesn't include restoration of your marriage? Ever? Am I truly everything you need? Will you continue to love Me, or will you walk away?"

Those early morning questions were as sharp as a two-edged sword.[57] Penetrating. Piercing. I felt a jab deep within the root system of my faith probing my thoughts and the attitude of my heart.[58] I felt I was choking on the same dust stirred up when Jesus asked His disciples, "Do you want to leave, too?"[59]

"With all the time we have spent together," God continued, "Will you now trust Me with your future? Do you spend time with Me because you love Me or to get what you want?"

I avoided answering by getting dressed, doing a few chores around the house, then running errands.

By the afternoon, I hadn't shaken God's intense scrutiny. When I opened my mailbox an official envelope from the Circuit Court was addressed to me with a notarized copy of the Final Decree of Divorce enclosed. God knew the papers were there! I couldn't bear to look at this legalized severance of my life. Sobbing, I cried, "God, why didn't You work it out *my* way! Why didn't You change my husband's heart? You said, 'The king's heart is like channels of water in the hand of the Lord; He turns it wherever He wishes.'[60] Lord, why? Isn't it *good* that marriages be restored? You said You hate divorce![61] I didn't want to be divorced! I didn't want to be forever branded with a big "D" across my breast! I didn't want to be an object of pity, suspicion, or even scorn!"

Then the Lord interrupted, "I have promised to give you My best. I have promised that I would not withhold any good thing from you. Donna, the man you married thirty years ago is not good for you now. His heart doesn't yearn for Me, and that is not good!"

"This day has been extremely difficult, Lord! I don't want to listen any more. I've had enough! If this is a class, then I want the bell to ring so I can leave!"

But God wasn't finished. Abruptly this verse came to my mind.

> "Be anxious for nothing, but in everything by prayer and supplication *with thanksgiving*, let your requests be made known to God; and the peace of God, which surpasses all understanding, will guard your hearts and minds through Christ Jesus" (Philippians 4:6, 7 NKJV, emphasis added).

"What was that? 'With thanksgiving'? How absurd! How could you ask that of me, Lord? I'm not sure I want to continue this discussion right now. *Give thanks*? Lord, this is too much!"

In the agonizing silence that followed, God shared His reasons for a thankful heart.

"Donna, it's easy to be thankful when the battle has *already* been won. Anyone can sing. I hear those songs of praise and thanksgiving quite often.

"And there are also times when you know a battle is coming. You've read the book of Joshua and saw the victories! I told Joshua that I had given Jericho into his hand and its king and the valiant warriors *before* the battle ever took place![62] Donna, I patiently wait for My children to apply those verses today. I want them to come to Me *before* their battles, expecting to see My victories. Not as many songs are heard.

"But the most precious songs I'll ever hear are sung in the *midst* of the battle. These melodies give evidence of the very pinnacle of believing faith from those who act out of obedience rather than feelings. Those hymns of praise that Peter sang in prison,[63] the songs from the lips of Paul and Silas[64] while their legs were stretched and their backs were bleeding, rhapsodized my Kingdom! You have no idea what celebration goes on when even one song is sung in the midst of a battle.

"Donna, in your tragedy you have sought me with your whole heart. You have cried out to Me in your despair. You have spent invaluable time with Me. And My Comforter has never left you. I want you to keep singing."

I don't know how long I sobbed. On my knees with my arms stretched out and my face buried in the bed, I couldn't leave. I stayed as long as it took for God to break through my unrelenting determination that if I prayed long and hard enough, if I trusted enough, and obeyed enough, then surely God would have to answer *my* prayer. I wanted to call it faith, but God defined it as coming to get what *I* wanted instead of trusting Him for what was best for me.

Broken, weak, and weary, I whispered, "Lord, I'm beginning to understand. The destruction of my marriage is something I *never* wanted. I didn't even want to say the word, much less *be* divorced. But because my husband chose to turn away, I have gotten to know You in a deeper and more intimate way. And for that, Lord, *I am thankful,* because You are worth it!"

> "For I know the thoughts that I think toward you, says the Lord, thoughts of peace and not of evil, to give you a future and a hope. Then you will call upon Me and go and pray to Me, and I will listen to you" (Jeremiah 29:11, 12 NKJV).

– Chapter Nineteen –

A Modern Parable

Lord, another lesson today? I still have so much to learn! When I think there couldn't possibly be any more spiritual muscles to stretch, You always find one or two that need more exercise. Stretching is learning, and learning brings more accountability to put into practice those things I know to do.

"Lord, I struggle with waiting, and I don't even know what I'm waiting for! In Psalm 27:14 David said, 'Wait on the Lord, be of good courage, and he shall strengthen your heart." Lord, how long do I wait? I still feel unsettled. I'm not comfortable in my job. I wrestle with whether I should look for another. And now that my marriage is over, I wonder whether I should stay here or move out of town. If I move, I would leave all my close friends, Lord, I'm not sure I could do that. Is all of this uncertainty for a reason? Am I on the right road, but just need to stay a little longer until You have worked out something else? Lord, I just don't know what to do."

I shared my struggle with my counselor, hoping he could help me sift through the rubble and find a new goal for my life.

In our discussion, he pointed out that waiting on God was good. It could become a time of tremendous spiritual growth. Then he began to share a modern-day parable about a carpenter he'd recently seen on a trip to historic Williamsburg.

In the woodworking shop, which had retained its colonial appearance, the carpenter demonstrated how the early settlers made wagon wheels. First, he cut strips for the outer rim and spokes from a supply of wood stacked in a corner of his shop. Then he shaped the hubs from wood that had been cut down and seasoned for several years. It was much stronger and less likely to split under pressure. The carpenter explained that the strength of the wheel depended upon the strength of the hub.

Cut down. Seasoned. Those were easy words to straddle. My thoughts wandered, personifying this once tender sapling. "That poor tree didn't know why it was chopped down. It was content growing with all the other trees, until one day someone took an ax to it! Now it lies on the ground looking up and asking why. I can identify with that! And when spring approached, it probably eyed with envy as his fellow trees shook off winter's cold and sprouted new and luscious leaves that would keep the forest cool and refreshing. If that weren't enough, it must have lamented over the fact that it didn't stand tall and sturdy anymore. It wasn't in the pictures the tourists took of the beautiful fall foliage.

"If trees could talk, this one would probably cry out, 'Why couldn't I have been left alone? Why couldn't I have continued to be a part of the forest? I'm no use! I have no life! I'm going to lie here and rot!'"

One advantage of voicing my struggle gave me an opportunity to hear what choices were available. I *could* consider waiting on God as a waste of time. I *could* blaze my own trail. To lie down and rot was easy. It cost nothing.

Or, I could choose, as my counselor encouraged, to wait on God.

If I waited on God, then He'd let me know if I should look for another job. If I waited on God, then He'd let me know if I should move. If I waited on God, He'd direct my steps. If I waited on the God, He'd strengthen my heart.

Even though I had no definitive plans, I decided to wait on God.

> "Whatever is true, whatever is noble, whatever is right, whatever is pure, whatever is lovely, whatever is admirable—if anything is excellent or praiseworthy—think about such things" (Philippians 4:8 NIV).

> "Being confident of this, that he who began a good work in you will carry it on to completion until the day of Christ Jesus" (Philippians 1:6 NIV).

~ Chapter Twenty ~

There Is Significance in Each Day

Those early morning commutes to my counselor's office were grueling. At 6 A.M. when the sun was barely peeping over the trees, the beltway was already bumper to bumper. Horns blasted to speed up or move over, only to slam on the brakes several feet ahead. An accident-ready-to-happen was around every bend as racers drove with open throttles to get to work on time.

But gridlock was this morning's traffic report from the helicopter overhead. It never failed. The fender-bender was only a half-mile from where I was stopped. Annoyed, I inched my way along, knowing I would be late for my appointment.

Finally reaching the office, I poured a cup of coffee as I unwound from the snarling traffic. This beltway madness helped depict my inner turmoil. I began our session, "I know God has intervened on my behalf in the past, but what about now? There are no scheduled court dates. No unsuspecting phone calls. Nothing painful has happened recently. I seem to be intact. I don't want to be misunderstood. I *am* thankful for all the things God has done for me, and I *am* aware of my basic needs He faithfully provides. My food, clothing, job and warm bed don't go unnoticed. Even Jesus said in Matthew 6 that life is more than food, and the body is more than clothing."

After a few more ramblings, I asked, "What significance is there in my life *now*? I don't want to live racing down life's road, only to discover myself sitting in a gridlock one day and realize that I'm headed toward nothing but nebulous insignificance!"

"Every day has significance," my counselor advised. "Life has significance because of God. You see, God can come any time He chooses. And it is significant that, as of today, He has withheld His coming. Therefore, you have another day in which you might see how He has manifested Himself to you."

I plopped my head back on the office wing chair and looked heavenward as I contemplated his answer. There was something convincingly powerful in his closing statement. I drove to work wondering how would my life be affected—no, *changed*—if I chose to look for God's involvement in my life every day.

Five o'clock couldn't have come sooner! Promptly I bounded for home, anxious to develop my morning's scribbled mental notes. With Bible and concordance opened on the kitchen table, I looked for examples of nebulous insignificance turned significant.

Ah-ha! Here's one. The march around Jericho found in the Old Testament book of Joshua, chapter six. God had declared victory over this fortified city for His people if they would follow His simple, uncomplicated plan.

No battering rams were needed. No mounding catapults, or piling up an arsenal of huge stones. No sophisticated war maneuvers were carried out in order to seize this city. It would be won by God's strategy and men's faith.

Those who lived behind Jericho's thick walls must have thought it strange when the troops fell in line. The march was headed up by armed men, followed by seven priests carrying seven trumpets of rams' horns, the ark of the Lord, and the rear guard.

"You shall march around the city, all the men of war circling the city once. You shall do so for six days," God had said. "On the seventh day you shall march around the city seven times, and the priests shall blow the trumpets." Then Joshua gave God's final order to his troops: "You shall not shout, nor let your voice be heard, nor let a word proceed out of your mouth, until the day I tell you, 'Shout!' Then you shall shout!" (Joshua 6:10).

I tried to imagine what those warriors might have thought as they adjusted their armor or tightened the straps on their sandals.

Monday. "That's it? Just walk and keep silent? What's so significant about that?"

Tuesday. "I'm not used to doing nothing. We're known throughout the region for our strength and victories! We don't need weapons to break through? How bizarre!" Dust was all that stirred. Nothing else.

Wednesday. A barrage of profaned jeers flowed and random bursts of laughter were heard from those who sat on top of the high walls. But no matter what was going on the troops kept marching.

Thursday. A somber cloud might have encircled the citizens of this fortified city. The eerie blasts from the rams' horns combined with the monotonous sound of marching feet may have begun to send chills up their spines.

Friday. Five days had passed and the unnerving silence went unbroken. Just the sound of marching and the blasts from rams' horns. Yet, nothing had happened. Significant? My natural response, "Hardly!"

Saturday. The sixth day of marching once around the perimeter, just as God had commanded. No directives from the military officer. Silence. The single-most compelling command. Significant?

Then came Sunday! "Finally!" they must have thought. "Yes! Seven times. Just as God has said!"

They obeyed God's command to the fullest. With the blast of trumpets and the shout from the soldiers, that massive wall was reduced to rubble! Unbelievable! What supernatural power was displayed before their eyes!

God!

Power!

Significant? Absolutely!

How did God manifest Himself to them on Monday? Tuesday? Wednesday through Saturday? He gave them the courage to obey and the strength to carry out His resolute plan that demanded obedience with every step.

Every day wasn't like the seventh. They had to keep on keeping on without another word from God. All they knew was that He had promised them victory. Had they not marched, had they not been silent, had they marched for six days instead of seven, there would have been no celebration.

Each dusty impression left by the sandals of those obedient warriors showed incalculable significance. Little did they know when they fell in line in the pre-dawn hours that they were but a step away from seeing one of Gods' most fantastic miracles. Regardless of whether or not they agreed with His plan, questioned along the way, or feared reprisal from those within the walls, it was significant that with each stride they cast an indelible footprint in the concrete of obedience.

"Every day has significance," I wrote in my journal. "There is one more day in which I might see how God has manifested Himself to me."

As I walk around the perimeter of my world, I don't know how God will manifest Himself to me, but it was *significant* when I didn't take lightly the Scripture, "...casting all your anxiety upon Him, because He cares for you" (I Peter 5:7b), before going to work last Tuesday. It softened the reprimand from one of my bosses.

The day I had my oil changed, a guy found a nail in the front right tire. I could have taken my car to any one of those speedy places, but I chose to take it to the garage close to work. It was God who pointed out the nail. That was significant!

As I started thumbing through my journal, I found more instances of what I used to consider inconsequential or insignificant, but they weren't insignificant after all. They were indelible impressions left by God to show me that He *had* been intimately involved in my life. He *had* manifested Himself to me. Now I look for God in my world each day. For I, too, might be one step away from a fantastic miracle God has prepared for me!

How secure I have become each night as I pull down the covers and crawl into bed. With my head on my pillow, I snuggle under my blanket and smile. "Lord, I saw You in my world today!" Breathing deeply, near the edge of sleep, I wonder what tomorrow will bring.

> "Whoever has my commandments and obeys them, he is the one who loves Me. He who loves Me will be loved by my Father, and I too will love him, and *show* myself to him" (John 14:21 NIV).

– Chapter Twenty-One –

Oh, No! Not My Lawnmower!

I awakened to a delightful spring morning. From my bedroom window I noticed how green the grass was getting and how tall it was growing. God had been so gracious to send help with my lawn when I had been weak and tired. But now, because I believed God had not led me to move yet, one of my newly acquired jobs was to take care of the lawn.

This morning I decided that "today is the day." Donning my work clothes and polishing my Harriet Homeowner badge, I unlocked the door to the tool shed and stared at the lawnmower.

Not wanting to look like a novice, I dragged the mower from the shed to the back of the house so the neighbors wouldn't see my flailing arms as I attempted to start it. With great anticipation, I pushed the prime button and yanked the cord with all my might. I didn't realize how excited I could get from a little sputter!

"Okay! Just one more good pull," I reasoned, "Then surely it will start!" With a yank hard enough to pull my shoulder out of socket, the motor sputtered again, but with less enthusiasm. I primed it again and yanked again. The result was the same pitiful cough.

"That's okay," I reassured myself. "I've probably flooded it!"

Taking a few minutes to cool down, I walked around the yard taking note of what needed to be done. I prayed, "Lord, I'm in need of You as my Husband.[65] If I had a husband, surely he could get my mower started. Lord, I'm asking You to help me with the mower."

Several more attempts were made, but to no avail. I was frustrated and disappointed. I wanted no pity, nor did I want my yard to be an embarrassment to the neighborhood. All I wanted was to be able to start my mower and God hadn't helped me. I gave up and walked across the street to borrow my neighbor's mower. I was thankful for the loan, but I wanted to be self-sufficient!

After cutting the grass and returning the mower, I tried to calmly think through what I should do. Knowing of a lawn-mower shop close by, I called to schedule a pick up.

"Okay, lady, we'll pick it up on Tuesday. It will take seven business days to service it and get it back to you."

"Fine," I replied.

"That's more like it. I *can* handle this!"

Tuesday I put the mower out on the deck before going to work, feeling confident that I was in control. As the windshield wipers cleared my vision when I drove up my driveway after work, the mower was still there, getting drenched! "Oh, no! Why didn't they come? Did this rain ruin it?"

Wednesday morning I called. "Why didn't you pick up my mower?"

"I'm sorry, lady, but our truck broke down. We won't be able to pick it up for several days. If you can bring it in, we can fix it in a couple of days; or we can reschedule another pickup after the truck is fixed."

I felt I had no other choice but to take it on Saturday. The spring rains were great for the lawns, but soaked my ego. For the next five days I watched the grass grow inch by inch. Every day I questioned why God had not helped. Saturday was going to be tight. A couple months earlier I had promised to help decorate the tables at church for a Women's Missions Brunch. But if I got an early start, I would have plenty of time to decorate, run home to change my clothes, then somehow get that albatross of a lawnmower into the trunk of my car!

Early Saturday morning, I rushed out of the driveway, my car loaded with baskets, fresh ivy and azalea blooms. The first to arrive at church, I quickly unloaded my car and began to fill the baskets with flowers. Other volunteers soon arrived ready to help with the ivy, ribbons and violets. Satisfied with our efforts, I hurriedly gathered up the twigs and dead blooms, anxious to make a quick exit. As I headed towards the door, I recognized the wife of a young missionary my son had stayed with in New Guinea while on a mission trip. I couldn't leave without saying hello.

That conversation led to another, and I ended up staying much longer than planned. The men's breakfast, which had been held on the other side of the thick vinyl curtain, had just ended. I was amused to watch the guys peep around the curtain and joke about the difference between their banal potted plants and the ivy, ribbons, and flowers.

After a few more minutes of light conversation, one of those men, the husband of a dear friend and an elder at the church, drew me aside.

"Who is mowing your lawn this summer?"

I looked at him in disbelief. "No one," I said blinking back the tears. "I'm able to do it, but I'm having trouble getting my lawnmower started."

Bob commented, "A couple of weeks ago God laid it on my heart to ask you about your lawn. Would you allow me to be obedient to God and minister to you by mowing your lawn this summer?"

I was shocked, blessed, excited, and humbled all at the same time! "I can't believe it!" I said. "If you only knew!"

Another revival took place in my car as I drove home. My heart was ecstatic! "God, I can't believe it! I can't believe how You knew my need all along and were arranging to have it met. Oh, God, I can never thank you enough!"

Monday morning, the receptionist at work buzzed me to pick up line four.

"This is Burke Mowing Service. Just wanted to let you know that our truck is fixed. When can we pick up your mower?"

"There's no need. But thanks anyway!"

With a smile and a chuckle, I hung up the phone, thinking about the expressions on their faces had they known why their truck had been on the fritz!

Once again I had much to write in my journal when Bob was outside mowing. "God," I began, "You have shown me how faithful You are. I wanted You to fix my lawnmower, but You had a better plan. You wanted to take care of my lawn, as my Husband would!"

During other times of reflections, if I'd ever start complaining about something else that needed to be done, God would say, "Speak up, Donna! I can't hear you over the roar of the mower!"

What joy and delight fills my heart as now I sing, "My God is an awesome God! He reigns from heaven above!"[66]

~ Chapter Twenty-Two ~

Rain

For days the skies dropped buckets of rain. Not only was it raining outside, but a storm was brewing within my soul. The dark clouds began rolling in after I had talked with each one of my children about their plans for the upcoming Fourth of July.

Strong winds picked up when Phil, my Texas son, shared that he and his family were going to his in-law's farm in Mississippi with other family members. Ominous rumblings continued upon hearing that Sharon in North Carolina had plans for a family picnic with her husband's family. Stacy and her husband, living in Delaware, were going to enjoy a day of golfing with her in-laws.

Lightning seared my heart as I stood drenched in this deluge of despair. I believed that all my children were now bonding with their spouses' families and I would end up being totally ignored and alone forever.

Family times like those of the Waltons danced in my head. I had always wanted *my* home to be the hub of activity, filled with warm fuzzies and apple pie. But now because of the painful memories, home must not be warm to them anymore.

"Oh, God, this is NOT what I wanted! This is NOT what I prayed for! Will my family just fade away like an old photograph? Will we become mere recollections of the past? Parched memories? With all my children cleaving to their spouses' families, do I fit in? It's so unfair! My home has been violated!" All my dreams of planning extended family vacations, sewing little dresses for my granddaughters, playing ball with my grandsons, or buying matching Easter outfits were nothing but smoldering ashes. "Lord, what is significant about this day?"

My intensified pain turned into intensified anger and that frightened me. I *knew* the consequences of anger. I had experienced it in my home growing up.

Looking for help, I picked up A. W. Tozer's little book, *The Pursuit of God* with its heavily worn, dog-eared, and highlighted pages. In Chapter Two, "The Blessedness of Possessing Nothing," I read, "The way to deeper knowledge of God is through the lonely valleys of soul poverty and abnegation of all things."[67] I asked God to clarify "abnegation of all things," or, as Paul says in Galatians 2:20, "crucifying or dying" to all my dreams. As I stretched out on the carpet with my arms extended, as if on a cross, tears rolled down the sides of my face as I struggled to pray. "Lord, how do you die? How do you die to people you love? How do you die to those lonely feelings? Lord, how do you give up everything that is precious? If I were dead, I would have no feeling. But Lord, I am alive and I *do* feel! Please help me understand."

A profane interruption assailed. "Give it up! Who do you think you are? You're no Tozer! Get a grip! Go downstairs and treat yourself to a bowl of that ice cream you bought at the store yesterday. Then you'll feel better. It will help you to forget about this. Don't get so out of touch with reality!"

Even though I didn't give in to the ice cream attack, the distraction was successful enough to get me off the floor. Yet all day I tried to understand what it meant to die to my deepest desires and, with open hands, give them to my Father. I went to bed with no closure to my struggle.

> "Truly, truly I say to you, unless a grain of wheat falls into the earth and dies, it remains by itself alone; but if it dies, it bears much fruit" (John 12:24 NASB).

I awakened early Sunday morning, went to church, then came straight home. A wave of familiar pangs flooded over me as I opened the kitchen door. I was also well aware that the joy I had experienced was waning. I wanted it back, but I couldn't shake this heaviness. It frightened me to think that I was slowly going back to square one in my walk with the Lord as anger and bitterness welled up inside. The accolades of past victories were slipping away.

Psalm 100 had joy and gladness in it, so I wrote it in my journal and circled all the "joy" words as I ate my salad alone.

> "Make a *joy*ful noise unto the Lord, all ye lands.
> Serve the Lord with *gladness*: come before His presence with *singing*.
> Know ye that the Lord he is God:
> it is he that hath made us and not we ourselves;
> we are his peoples, and the sheep of his pasture.
> Enter into his gates with *thanksgiving*,
> and into his courts with *praise*:
> be *thankful* unto him, and *bless his name*.
> For the Lord is *good*; his mercy is everlasting;
> and his truth endureth to all generations" (Psalm 100 KJV, emphasis added).

I joined my Bible Study group after a long Sunday afternoon. All seven friends could tell something was wrong. "Donna, this is not like you!" Marguarite observed. Jody, Sharon, and LaRose agreed. I shared the conversations I'd had with my children. Everyone, including the guys, exhorted mildly in no uncertain terms, "You've got to give them up!

You've got to let them go!" I'd heard that before. Why must I have to give up my children, too? They were all I had left! I felt like I had been sent to the wood shed; but deep down inside I knew they were right!

On my way home that evening, my heart was heavier still. I pulled down the covers, plumped up the pillows behind my back, crossed my arms and stared at the wall. I wasn't sleepy. Usually at times like this I would be on my knees, but I didn't feel like it. I didn't want to pray. I wiggled my feet back and forth under the covers, acting like a kid in an adult body. I opted to do other than what I knew to do. My childish actions drew me down Memory Lane.

When I was a little girl, my family would go to the country for weekend getaways. My dad and his siblings built a cabin to serve as a mutual gathering place. My family was part of the "city folk," so we stayed in the cabin with other out-of-town relatives.

A big gate which secured the cabin with a looped rope on a fence post opened up a world of adventure for my sister and me. When we arrived, we begged to ride the gate like a horse when our dad unlatched it. With delightful squeals of "yahoo" and a "giddy-up," we giggled as we waited for the gate to "buck" against a rock that stopped its swing. Happily, we jumped off the gate and race each other toward the cabin, looking forward to good times that lay ahead.

As I scooted down in the bed a little more to rest my head, I thought about being a child once again, but now swinging atop heaven's gate. The Lord had given me permission. I could swing there all day if I wanted because I was His child. But swinging on His gate didn't bring the excitement or giggles like it had in the country because I was lugging around a heavy burden. I felt like Christian in John Bunyan's, *Pilgrim's Progress*, except I was already in the Celestial City.

"What have you got there?" asked the Lord. He looked into my sack and saw the anger, bitterness, and self-pity. It reeked, permeating the air.

"Donna, let it go! I don't want you dragging that horrible stench through My courts. There is so much here for you to enjoy without it. You can explore all the crevasses in my holy places and find blessings with your name on them. I want you to have joy. I want you to worship Me with gladness. I want you to giggle! To laugh and be free! You don't have to be lonely and afraid. My Spirit will empower you to overcome your anger, bitterness and self-pity. But you have to let go.

"And your dreams…don't keep them in a box. Open it up and give them to Me. Allow Me to fill your emptiness. That's what 'abnegation of all things' is about!"

"Lord, it's so hard to let go—especially my children's hearts! Next to letting my husband go, this is the hardest thing I've had to do!"

I thought how foolish it would be to try to manipulate my children's hearts or make them feel guilty when they didn't respond the way *I* wanted them to. That would only cause more pain for all of us. They would resent me. If I held them too tightly, I could suffocate the love that we share.

"Lord, I can't win! If I don't give them to You, I will end up a bitter old woman. I don't want that. So I *must* release them. You know how much I love them. If loving means letting go, then I *must.*

"And Lord, if it is too hard for them to come home, then I will go to them. I will go so that I might bless them, expecting nothing in return. Lord, everyday I will pray for them. Everyday I will entrust their hearts to You."

And with that, I fluffed my pillow and lay down.

"Good night, Father. I think I can sleep now."

– Chapter Twenty-Three –

Don't Walk on Thin Ice

It started with a card. Just a simple card. Not elaborate or conspicuous, but tucked in an ordinary white envelope. An old basket once used for canning jars now held heartfelt expressions from so many. I'd chosen to believe that each one was God's way of giving me a hug. So it wasn't unusual to receive a card today with no return address. As I tore open the envelope while standing by the mailbox, embers of astonishment and excitement sparked my emotions. It was from a man I had recently met. When he learned about my situation, he had been noticeably moved with compassion.

Within the few seconds it took to walk back into the house, a fortress of countless thoughts and emotions began to build. The clock ticked away seconds, minutes, and ultimately an hour as I sat frozen in my kitchen chair staring at this card. I laid it down only to pick it up again to read and reread every word. Suggestive ideas yelled from their now secured lofty places in my mind.

"Does this card deliver something more than encouragement?" I didn't want to think how wrong I was to entertain such a thought. Rather, I preferred to be mesmerized with the idea that someone outside my normal circle of friends had considered me *interesting.* That felt good. My husband had thrown me away like unwanted trash. I tried to substantiate my reasons for massaging this fantasy because this man valued me enough to send a card.

Truth began. "Look, the card was only a nice gesture. That's all. It was just one of the many thoughtful and encouraging responses you have already received."

Lies interjected, "No! It was more than that!"

Truth responded, "It was nothing more than a friendly expression of concern."

"Never!" Lies exclaimed. "You need to take this opportunity to thank him for the card and his kindness. It could spark a special interest. That attention would be good after your rejection."

Truth, aware of this stronghold,[68] warned, "You don't need to approach him. You need to stay away. Your vulnerability for such attention is at a peak."

Truth was right. I was *extremely* vulnerable!

"I'm afraid that just as Eve was deceived by the serpent's cunning, your mind may somehow be lead astray from your sincere and pure devotion to Christ,"[69] Truth cautioned.

This encounter with the card opened up a whole new world of temptation I had never experienced before. Why was I struggling with this? Deep down I really didn't want to disobey what God had clearly said in His word. I knew what I *should* have done. I *should* have taken captive every thought to make it obedient to Christ,[70] but this strong irresistible pull to be special to someone was like a magnet that lifts demolished cars or steel beams. *My* power against such thoughts was impotent. The human desires that God created in me screamed out that *I* was in control of my life. Why should I have to obey God to get them met? Like a damsel in distress, I longed for a prince to take me away.

Throughout the day, my fantasies and illusions kept getting tangled up with truth and reality. I didn't try to separate them. I went to bed concurring in my loneliness that the special attention I craved could somehow be met through a blasé encounter with one whom was *not* God's best: He was married.

Caffeine boosted my awareness of a new day, a clean slate, *new mercies*[71] as God defined it, from yesterday's mail. As I sipped my first cup of coffee, trying to avoid the challenge that was looming over my morning—to see how God would manifest Himself today—I cleaned off the kitchen counter. As I walked through the family room to get a dust cloth, a shout from the radio stopped me.

"Don't walk on thin ice," this fiery Dallas preacher warned. "If you want to go ice fishing in the middle of a lake and you're not sure how thick the ice is, then *don't go there*!" He punctuated with his loud passionate voice. "If you're a recovering alcoholic, *stay away from bars*! If you're confronted by druggies, *go home a different way*! If you're struggling with something that can lead you down a wrong path, *run away*! Only you, God, and your enemy know your weakest link!"

His words were quick and to the point. Drowning in a sea of conviction, I listened as my dust cloth stirred up more dust than it collected. The god of this world *had* targeted my weakest link! I shook the bars of my imprisoned cell that I had willingly entered yesterday, then fell into a heap on the floor.

"God, it's so unfair! It's so hard!" I confessed. "I liked the feelings I had when that person reacted compassionately to my plight. He seemed to have felt my pain. My husband didn't think I was good enough, but this man must see value in me!"

Then a bucket of cold reality slapped me in the face. "God, what's wrong with me? I am struggling with the same thing that brought *me* so much pain!"

I felt as if I had been maimed by a huge cat that was amusing himself with my efforts to escape. With a sinister grin, he batted me around with his paw, waiting to claim his prey.

"God, if I don't escape, I'll be one more statistic whom the world will mock! And my children…what about my children? I would never be able to look in their faces again and say that You are sufficient. I would be a mockery to what I believe. My life would have no power, no purpose anymore!"

I took several deep breaths before I could gain composure from the inconsolable sobbing. Lovingly, God waited for me to stop then reached down with His hand of mercy to help me up. Then He told me why I needed *Him* to fight this battle.

"Satan wants to destroy you, Donna. He hates you. He gained a stronghold in your marriage and tore it apart. Now he desires to have you. He wants to render you powerless. He will try to kill, steal, and destroy[72] anyone who will follow him. Listen! His plans are evil. He will exploit you. He doesn't want you to use My power to say no to his evil plan. He doesn't love you, Donna, but I love you deeply."

"Father, *You* are my power to say no! Oh, God, I don't want to disobey You! I don't want You to come looking for me, only to find me curled up in a cold abandoned corner of hopelessness. Help me resist my enemy! I've got to do it *now*!"

This was one of the hardest battles I'd ever encountered. Unfortunately, that magnetic pull of wanting to be special to someone didn't lose its power overnight. The next morning my car became a closet where I put on God's armor so I could face another inevitable battle. I prayed that I would use His power within me[73] to hold up the sword that God had given me when lies seemed more appealing than truth. I decided to walk on the other side of the street, away from a tempting pitfall. And if I were tempted like that again, I prayed that I would be content with God's solitary companionship.

God used that time to teach me how deadly it can be to be carried away and enticed by my own desires.[74] The natural sequence that could have followed would have ultimately brought forth death[75] to my relationship with Him, my family, and friends. How thankful I am that God exposed how harmful it would be to try to satisfy my human longings[76] apart from Him, how it would have caused more pain. I could trust Him to bring someone into my life if that was His best for me.

A. W. Tozer poignantly zeroed in on the choices of an average man. "Let the average man be put to the proof on the question of who or what is above, and his true position will be exposed. Let him be forced into making a choice between God and money, between God and men, between God and personal ambition, God and self, God and human love, and God will take second place every time. However the man may protest, the proof is in the choices he makes day after day throughout his life."[77]

After this battle was over, God lovingly draped His mantle of compassion over me as we walked away together.

> "Blessed be the Lord, who daily bears our burden,
> The God who is our salvation.
> God is to us a God of deliverances;
> And to God the Lord belong escapes from death"
> (Psalm 68:19, 20).

– Chapter Twenty-Four –

New Construction

In the twenty-ninth chapter of the Old Testament book of I Chronicles, King David's heart was overflowing with joy. Supplies to build a temple for God's glory had been generously donated by David and all the people. "It will be exceedingly magnificent, famous and glorious throughout all lands,"[78] King David announced. Adulation sprang up in the hearts of everyone. Solomon, King David's son, would superintend the construction. How exciting this time must have been!

When people overheard the workers talk about the plans, exhilaration must have spread like wildfire. According to the blueprints, gold was everywhere: on the walls, inlaid in the floors, and over the doors. Gold cherubim would stand as sentries on either side of the ark.[79] Silver, brass, and bronze, together with iron, cedar, and marble were part of the structure. Courtyards would glisten with inlaid precious stones. A beautiful veil with an artistic design would be woven with blue, purple, and scarlet threads.[80] One thousand years later, that veil would be torn in two the hour Jesus died.

Upon completion, the splendor and grandeur must have been absolutely indescribable. As the sun shone over this completed temple, the precious metals must have glistened more brilliantly than the brightest fireworks on the Fourth of July! Perhaps it was a glimpse of the majesty and splendor of heaven.

King David, now late in years, praised the Lord in the sight of all the assembly because "...the people had offered so willingly, for they made their offering to the Lord with a whole heart" (I Chronicles 29:9).

> "Praise be to you, O Lord, God of our father Israel, from everlasting to everlasting. Yours, O Lord, is the *greatness* and the *power* and the *glory* and the *majesty* and the *splendor*, for everything in heaven and earth is yours. Yours, O Lord, is the kingdom; you are exalted as head over all.
> "Wealth and honor come from you; you are the ruler of all things. In your hands are strength and power to exalt and give strength to all. Now, our God, we give you thanks, and praise your glorious name" (I Chronicles 29:11, 12 NIV, emphasis added).

These verses seemed to shout, "Look at God! There is greatness, power, glory, victory, and majesty. This is who He is! But look one more time. Look at what He offers. Power! Strength! It's right there in His hands. He has power to make men great and to strengthen everyone!"

God held out His open hands and asked, "Donna, I have within My hands power that will make you great for My sake. Won't you ask Me for what I want so much to give you?"

This is the God to whom I come! It is to Him I bring the heaviness of my heart. This *God* meets with me and listens, speaks to my heart through His Word and His Spirit. It is to this God I have cried in my pain, "God, please help me. Fill my loneliness. Strengthen me.

"Just as David lifted his hands and praised You, so I lift my hands to You, *my Living God!* I don't stand before heaps of great wealth, as David, but broken pieces of my life.

"Lord, what is Your blueprint for me? I want You to rebuild my life. Take the pieces and make me into a temple who honors You! Pour a new foundation from Your love, joy, and peace. Hew beams with Your power so that I will stand victoriously. Cover me with a tapestry woven from threads of kindness, gentleness and praise!"[81]

> "Who is like the Lord our God, Who is enthroned on high, Who humbles Himself to behold the things that are in heaven and in the earth? *He raises the poor from the dust, And lifts the needy from the ash heap*, To make them sit with princes, With the princes of His people. He makes the barren woman abide in the house as a joyful mother of children. Praise the Lord" (Psalm 113:5-9 NASB, emphasis added).

– Chapter Twenty-Five –

In the Throne Room with God

A radio sermon had challenged me to linger after prayer instead of getting up off my knees right away. "Have pencil and paper and be prepared to stay a while," this pastor encouraged.

So one afternoon after I had spent some time on my knees, I sat down on the bedroom floor with my journal and pen in hand and waited. Smiling, I remembered the story about Elijah and the widow's jars of oil in the Old Testament. Elijah had instructed a penniless widow to "go around and ask all your neighbors for empty jars. Don't ask for just a few. Then go inside and shut the door behind you and your sons. Pour oil into all the jars, and as each is filled, put it to one side."[82] She kept filling jars, the Bible stated, until there were no jars left. Then the oil stopped flowing. We're not told how many jars she ultimately filled, but there was enough oil to sell so she could pay off her debts and still have money to live on. Like the widow, I had plenty of paper in my journal for God to fill. I also needed an extra measure of His grace to forgive *my* debtor as well as a large portion to live on.

As time ticked away, this communion brought portions of Scripture I'd not thought about nor noticed before. Three challenges surfaced as I lingered in the throne room with God.

"Donna," He warned me, "The enemy will continually try to discourage you. This warning is not for today, but every day. There will always be temptations and lies that Satan will use to try to distract you from seeking Me. You might as well expect it; he targets those who are on their knees. Satan has asked to sift you as wheat. *But I have prayed for you* that your faith would not fail."[83]

Believing that Jesus was deeply concerned about my faith brought reverence to these cloistered moments. I couldn't leave. Upon finding Jesus' prayer in the book of John, chapter 17, I put my name on the lips of the Son of God as He knelt before the Father and prayed.

"Father, I pray for [Donna]. You have given [her] to Me. My prayer is not that You take [her] out of the world, but that You protect [her] from the evil one. Father, just as You are in Me and I am in You, may [she] also be in Us so that *the world may believe* that You have sent Me. Father, I want [her], and [she] is one You have given Me, to be with Me where I am, and to see My glory, the glory You have given Me because You loved Me before the creation of the world."

As if His prayer acknowledged my presence, Jesus continued, "Donna, I pray that when you walk through fiery trials, you would hold onto the truths I left for you in My Word. I pray that you will trust My Spirit to be your Comforter and to empower you with victory over the very one I conquered through My death. I pray that you will not deny the power you have through Me by faith. I know you can't see Me, but trust what I tell you in My Word."

I turned another page in my journal and wrote down another truth that intertwined with the one just observed.

"I want you to glorify Me."

"Glorify!? Lord, I used to think that people glorified You when things were going well. David glorified your name throughout the earth. He was a king. He had a platform from which to praise you. I'm no king! I have no crown nor platform! Glorify? Lord, help me understand."

"Donna, do you love Me? Do you really love Me? With all your heart?"

"Lord, you asked Peter those same questions. Then You told Peter, 'I tell you the truth, when you were younger, you dressed yourself and went where you wanted, but when you are old, you will stretch out your hands and someone else will dress you and lead you where you do not want to go. Jesus said this to indicate the kind of death by which Peter would *glorify* God. Then he said to him, "Follow Me"' (John 21:18, 19 NIV, emphasis added).

"Lord, You knew that Peter would die a very painful death! He was stretched out and crucified upside down, scholars tell us. And yet in his death Peter would *glorify* You. And then You added, 'Follow Me.' Lord, that must have been so hard!

"Are You glorified when Your children depend on You during the painful and difficult things in life? If so, then I, too, want to glorify You. I will follow You."

Lastly, God asked that I *remember all that He had done for me.*

King David sat before the Lord and asked, "Who am I, O Sovereign Lord…that you have brought me this far?" (II Samuel 7:18). Overwhelmed that he was part of God's mighty plans for his generation and generations to come, David took time to worship God.

Did he recall as a young boy the cold and lonely nights he gazed into the fire, poking it with a stick and watching the colored sparks fly, as he guarded his father's sheep? Or did he hum one of the songs he used to sing to God while lying on his back looking up at the stars?

What about the time Samuel, a renowned prophet of God, visited his father's house in search for the next king? Rumor had it that David's father, when Samuel inquired if there were other sons, nonchalantly admitted, "Oh, yes, I almost forgot, I *do* have another son. David. But he's only a shepherd boy. He's out in the field. You want me to send for him?"

Or was he lost in thoughts about the times he wrestled with a bear and a lion?

Facing Goliath was another story. Defeat seemed inevitable. His own brothers and countrymen were stymied with fear! With God's confidence and strength girding him, this small shepherd boy walked out from those fields that had become his sanctuary into a blinding glare of human weakness.

"Who do you think you are?" they smirked, jabbing each other in the ribs as David stepped forward to face Goliath alone. Those same brothers who had once ignored him were now chiding him for his boldness. But David's unquestionable faith allowed God to use him as an instrument of His power. Goliath fell with one blow from young David's small slingshot. Look what God accomplished through David on that day! And it all started on those cold and lonely hills as David desired to know God.

As I poked at the charred remains of my marriage, I remembered the place I'd been and how far God had brought *me.*

"Lord, I remember the days after my abandonment when close friends took me out-of-town so I could escape the stares, the questions and the suspicions. I remember the fear as I stood alone in a hotel room, so weak and unable to eat. In the blurred midnight hours I sang 'Great is Thy Faithfulness' with a tear-stricken voice. The song came ever so faintly from within the frail, broken skeleton of a rejected wife, but it came. Lord, where did it come from?"

"Donna, My Spirit bore witness with your spirit that you are My child!"[84]

"*You* implanted that song in my heart!"

"Donna, that simple, powerful song, full of truth, was given to you by My Spirit to relay My message to your heart. That was all that you could take in at the time. And when that chorus came out of your choking tearful heart, it was as though a full chorale accompanied by a symphonic orchestra resounded throughout the heavens! The angels rejoiced around the throne of grace at the magnificence of that song!"

"Lord, I remember facing the pressures of a new job. I remember the wrenching in my heart when alone I flew to greet my first grandchild. I remember the confusion and disruption that came with the knowledge of my mom's Alzheimer's disease. I remember how numb we all were at my younger daughter's wedding when it wasn't shared with her dad. I remember my sister asking me to take her son should the doctors find her cancer terminal. I remember that temptation when I could have lost everything!

"The air conditioner and an unexpected root canal were challenges that topped my heavy load. Lord, I needed You so much! I needed Your strength. I needed Your comfort, and I needed Your power to stand. And You were there supplying my every need.

"Lord, had I not gone through this "day of trouble," I could never have testified how You sheltered me in the secret place of Your tent. I would have never known the protection when You lifted me up on a rock. I would have never known Your strength that enabled me to stand. I would never have magnified You in my midnight. *Thank You, Lord, for bringing me this far!*"

> "For who is God besides the Lord?
> And who is the Rock, except our God?
> It is God who arms me with strength and makes my way perfect.
> He makes my feet like the feet of a deer and enables me to stand on the heights.
> He trains my hands for battle; my arms can bend a bow of bronze
> You give me your shield of victory, You stoop down to make me great.
> You broaden the path beneath me, so that my ankles do not turn" (II Samuel 22:23-27, 51 NASB).

~ Chapter Twenty-Six ~

A Vessel Fit for a King

While shopping for a birthday gift at the mall, the brightness of one particular store caught my eye as I walked by. I stopped and looked twice to see if the sun were shining in, even though I knew that stores in the mall had no windows. Every piece of merchandise was polished to perfection. A silver tea service glistened from the center of a glossy cherry table. Sparkling brass candlesticks and exquisite silver bowls added regal splendor to every piece of furniture. As the air circulated, lights from an overhead chandelier reflected on the finishes.

I sauntered around this seemingly majestic setting, gliding my fingertips along the waxed tables, as if an invited guest to a palace. I looked around to see if anyone else was drawn into the store by such brilliance. This place was fit for a king!

After purchasing a gift, I grabbed a quick bite at a fast food place on my way home. Recouping from what seemed to be at least a mile's walk through the mall, I plopped down on the couch with a book in hand. It had tweaked my interest for no other reason than the title, *When God Interrupts...Finding*

New Life Through Unwanted Change. The subject seemed weighty for such a small book. Settling into a comfortable position, I was curious to read what Craig Barnes had to say.

Chapter titles jumped out as I flipped through the pages. "Abandoned by Success." "Abandoned by Health." "Abandoned by Family." "Abandoned by God." In chapter three, "A Place You'd Rather Not Go," Barnes said, "One of the most frustrating things about Jesus is that He just won't settle down. He is constantly moving us away from the places where we would prefer to stay, like Galilee, and moving us closer to Jerusalem, where we do not want to go."[85]

I scanned the Gospels to find out what happened in Galilee, then recorded each event in my journal. God sent the angel Gabriel to announced to Mary, from Nazareth of *Galilee*, that she was to give birth to the Son of the Most High (see Luke 1:26,32). It was in the villages in *Galilee* where Jesus taught in the synagogues and everyone praised him (see Luke 4:14). Across the lake from *Galilee*, Jesus healed the demon-possessed man who was living among tombs (see Luke 8:26). The wedding where Jesus turned water into wine was at Cana which is in *Galilee* (see John 2:1-11). Jesus appeared to his disciples after his resurrection…in *Galilee* (see Matthew 28:10). Things happened in Galilee!

It wasn't so in Jerusalem. Jesus wept over Jerusalem. "O Jerusalem, Jerusalem, the city that kills the prophets and stones those sent to her! How often I wanted to gather your children together, just as a hen gathers her brood under her wings, and you would not have it" (Luke 13:34 NASB).

To ponder Jerusalem made me uncomfortable, admitting that Galilee was where I'd rather stay. Jerusalem was a hard place. Jesus was stripped of everything in Jerusalem. He completely yielded to the will of His Father in Jerusalem. Jesus died in Jerusalem.

But Jerusalem is also a place of transformation. A new kind of life awaits those who journey there, on the other side of the cross. Jerusalem is where I exchange everything *I* want for everything *He* wants for me! While there, I admitted how hot the flames were when I was publicly humiliated and ashamed as I faced every church member.

Jesus responded, "I've also been shamed and humiliated."[86]

"Lord, the day my husband called—eight months after he left—I thought our marriage was going to be restored. But after a few hours, he walked away, again."

"Many people walked away from Me, too,[87] Donna. I understand."

"That New Year's Eve, Lord...the solitude was deafening!"

"I've felt loneliness. 'Foxes have holes and birds of the air have nests, but the Son of Man has no place to lay his head.'[88] Yes, I know."

While in Jerusalem I wrote down what Peter told his brothers and sisters in Christ who, under the hand of Nero, were used as human torches to light up his garden.

> "In this [I] greatly rejoice, even though now for a little while, if necessary, [I] have been distressed by various trials, that the proof of [my] faith, being more precious than gold which is perishable, even though tested by fire, may be found to result in praise, and glory and honor at this revelation of Jesus Christ; and though [I] have not seen Him, [I] love Him, and though [I] do not see Him now, but believe in Him, [I] greatly rejoice with joy inexpressible and full of glory, obtaining as the outcome of [my] faith the salvation of [my] soul" (I Peter 1:6-9 NASB).

Jerusalem is where God burns away my impurities—those unhealthy habits, unrealistic expectations, and unyielding spirit that get in His way. As I stayed, the Lord comforted my past hurts. "I heard your every painful cry, Donna. Yes, you were distressed by many trials; but a process was going on. In that fire, your Refiner's fire, your faith grew stronger as I burned away the impurities that mar your beauty. My heat was not too hot to destroy, but hot enough to be effective.

"I promise that one day you are going to be a part of the celebration of My praise, honor, and glory! One day, even though you have not seen Me, yet you have loved Me and believed in Me, you shall greatly rejoice with joy inexpressible![89] Did you catch My words 'rejoice,' 'joy,' and 'inexpressible?' I gave those words to Peter because there was no other way to adequately describe all that is waiting for those who love Me!

"Donna, I make no apology for the Refiner's fire. Now your life will shine more brilliantly for Me. I make no apology for lovingly squeezing you in order to produce the fruit from My vine so that others may be refreshed and encouraged. The Refiner's fire and the crushed fruit have made you fit for the King's use!"

> "But who can endure the day of His coming? And who can stand when He appears?
> For He is like a refiner's fire and fullers' soap.
> And He will sit as a smelter and purifier of silver, and He will purify [Donna] and refine [her] like gold and silver, so that [she] may present to the Lord offerings in righteousness" (Malachi 3:2, 3 NASB).

– Chapter Twenty-Seven –

Forgiven

Saturdays were hard, especially in the summer. I usually spent Saturdays running errands and doing light cleaning or menial yard work. But this Saturday it was too hot to do anything, which made the day seem even longer. My thoughts wandered back to the snapshot of advice I gave the previous Thursday night when I shared with the "twenty-something" Bible study group. "God is there for the lonely. Use those times to seek Him. Act on the fact that God has inked your name in His appointment book and that He will be expecting you!"

Yes, I knew what to do. With good intentions, I sat down on the sofa, bowed my head, and prayed, "Lord, here I am again. You know my struggle on this hot, sultry Saturday. I have no plans, no invitations to visit anyone. What can I do today? What is the significance of this day?"

I played tapes, which were getting a little warped, hoping to fill this empty feeling. I waited until the afternoon when the heat index dropped, then, out of boredom, cleared out the dead leaves that had collected behind the tool shed and swept off the deck. No one was out, not even the dogs!

After a cool shower, I turned on the television—which I seldom did—and joined the ranks of couch potatoes. Nothing interested me as I surfed through my minimal allotment of channels, until I intercepted a live courtroom scene. Because I was working in a law firm, the dynamics of a legal encounter captured my attention.

The courtroom drama was about a prisoner who had served fifteen years on death row for killing a man. He was appealing his verdict, before a jury, to change his sentence from an eventual death in the electric chair to a life sentence. My interest peaked when I heard that his heinous crime had taken place on January 10. My husband left me on that same day. Now I was intrigued.

The defense attorney called credible witnesses on the prisoner's behalf. One by one they told how the prisoner had touched his life from within the prison walls. An enlisted man, on his way to Saudi Arabia, shared how this prisoner had given him a reason to live after his wife said she would not be waiting for him when he returned. An old high school friend, whose life was in shambles, had been encouraged through his letters. Declarations of value continued with the prison chaplain. There was definitely something different about him.

The opposing counsel called the prisoner to the stand. He picked up a lead pipe and reenacted the blow which had caused death. The inmate bent over in the chair crying as he put his face in his hands. So penitent, he was barely audible when he testified how wrong he had been. He knew that he had inflicted excruciating and unnecessary pain as his victim lay dying. He understood that he should be punished for his crime. "If I live," he confessed, "It will be because of the mercy of the court."

A clinical psychiatrist reported her findings concerning the background of the one whose life hung in abeyance. His young life had been difficult and extremely painful, she testified. From his earliest memories, he had been victimized in his own home. He was unloved and had been sexually abused. At the age of twelve he felt like unwanted trash after a relative handed him over for foster care.

The prisoner was recalled by the defense attorney. Even though he had experienced tremendous trauma in his early life, with great clarity he testified, "I am without excuse for what I have done."

His statement astounded me. He could have used all kinds of excuses for his behavior, especially following the psychiatrist's report. There truly was something different about him.

After closing remarks from both attorneys, the jury retired to deliberate. During that time, a TV interviewer spoke with the inmate. "What do you have to say?"

He answered, "One day I would like to have an opportunity to talk to the daughter of the man I killed."

To that, the interviewer scoffed, "So you can say 'I'm sorry?'"

"No," he said, "What I did is beyond saying I'm sorry. When I took the stand, I looked briefly over at the daughter. It hurt so much to look at her—even for a few seconds—knowing what I had done to her father. But in that quick glance, I didn't see anger. I saw pain. I caused her pain and I must live with that."

Why was I so involved? Was I comparing two painful events just because they happened on the same day? I'm sure that was a small part in the beginning, but I didn't want to measure my pain against one who lost his life. There was no comparison. But there was something I believe God wanted me to see.

I saw brokenness, repentance, grief, and admission of guilt. I watched him struggle for composure as he owned up to it all. He was a living example of repentance. All he could do was ask for mercy.

When the jury returned, mercy was extended. The program ended.

Mercy. We get what we don't deserve.

There must be pain in the life of the one who imposed suffering on me. So I knelt down and prayed for the one who had caused my pain. I prayed that he, too, will be broken and repentant, seeking forgiveness from those he hurt so deeply. I will continue to pray that his heart will cry out, "God have mercy on me!" For only God knows true repentance; only He can interpret the meaning of one's heart.

This, I believe, was significant!

> "Have mercy upon me, O God, according to thy lovingkindness: according unto the multitude of thy tender mercies blot out my transgressions. Wash me thoroughly from mine iniquity, and cleanse me from my sin" (Psalm 51:1, 2 KJV).

– Chapter Twenty-Eight –

The Beautiful, Magnificent Rose

Grandchildren. What a blessing! In the past three years, I have been blessed with four, and more are on the way! It was fun taking them to the park and watching all the children play. Their imaginations were contagious. A little boy pressed his chin to his chest as he marched. A little girl happily "played like" mom, chattering and swinging her doll with great care. One child discovered a flower underneath a pile of leaves. To him it was a treasure. I overheard him telling the flower, "When Daddy brings flowers to Mommy, she is s-o-o-o happy!" Now he had the opportunity to do the same! His effervescence spilled over on all who watched from the park bench. With the agility of his small fingers, he pulled up this little flower, roots and all. His little face beamed with delight. He hid this limping flower behind his back until he was ready for the big moment. With the thrill of delight and anticipation of hugs and kisses, he presented his treasure saying, "Here, Mom. I picked this just for you!"

I looked at Paul's prayer for the believers in Ephesus. It unfolded like petals on a rose. There was an exciting potential ready to be discovered in its unfolding. According to Paul, I needn't miss out on the unfathomable riches Christ wants to share with me. There's no need to continually live in despair. According to this prayer, life can be bursting with hope. God will give me "exceeding abundantly above all that I could ever ask or think."[90]

Ephesians 3:14–21 NASB

> "For this reason I bow my knees before the Father, from whom his whole family in heaven and on earth derives its name…"

"I bow my knees before the Father." In humility, I bow before my loving Father who wants the best for me. I pray, not as if I'm looking down, shuffling my feet, and hoping that if I ask ever so faintly He will hear me and grant what I pray. No! I come boldly, with confidence[91] before His Throne of Grace.[92]

I can come to my Father, not on my own merits, but because of Christ. I can call Him Father because Christ made it possible when he willingly shed His blood for me.[93] Now I can approach my Father, cleansed[94] and pure. I come because Jesus is the Way, the Truth and the Life, and no man comes unto the Father except through Him.[95]

I gently pull back the next petals, looking for more truth.

> "I pray that out of his glorious riches He may strengthen you with power through his Spirit in your inner being…"

I asked for what my Father will lavish upon those who ask: His power. I have no power within me, but God is the power I need. Saying the words does not create power, it comes as I abide with Him.

"Lord, I need Your power to walk away from those painful days that could keep me in bondage until I die. I need

Your power to reach toward what lies ahead, to press on toward the goal for the prize of Your upward call in Christ Jesus."[96]

As more petals unfold, my heart becomes more challenged as I ask Christ to dwell in my heart through faith.

"Lord, I come before You because I believe You. I want You to expose the attitude of my heart. I want You to abide with me, take up residence, and clean out those areas that remain hidden."

As I spent that time with the Lord, He began to bring to my mind those things that I needed to clean out or let go. Knowing about areas in my life that need to change was one thing, but taking the time to stay with the Lord until I agreed with Him was not as easy. Time spent with God gave me the opportunity to change my heart about many things.

As still other petals opened, completing the full beauty of this flower, I was eager to pray that I, being rooted and established in love, may have power, together with all the saints, to grasp how wide and long and high and deep is the love of Christ, and to know the love that surpasses knowledge.

"Lord, if I am rooted and grounded in Your love, investing my time with You, if I walk in the truth of what I know, then I can grasp with the rest of the believers Your immeasurable love! I don't want to hope for victory others have had as I listen to their stories. I want Your victory to be lived out in me! I want to be included in the celebration of Your love!"

More petals declare:

> "...that I may be filled to the measure of all the fullness of God."

As I experience that love, I am filled to overflowing with the fullness of God in my life. I may not be able to describe adequately what that "fullness" looks like, but I know how it feels. When God fills, I have indescribable joy. He has given me boldness I have never had before. I can stand straight and tall, knowing that whatever the battle, I've already won! His filling is continuous, never-ending, never empty. Floodgates cannot contain the immeasurable love of Christ that flows through me.

I want my prayer to be sweet incense that surrounds the living God who sits on His throne. I want to offer Him one rose petal at a time, as I thank Him for Who He is and for what He has already done in my life. I don't want to miss out on all that He is going to do that I have yet to see!

Like that child who was bubbling because of the anticipated hugs and kisses in response to what he gave, so I anticipate with joy how God will respond to the praise I give Him. My prayer may be missing a few petals or the stem may be bent, but with joy I can bring the worship that is welling up inside of me and present it to my Father, saying, "Here, Lord, I prayed this just for You!"

It's just like God to say, "Thank you for your rose, Donna. I enjoyed the sweet aroma from your heart. And now, because I love you, I want you to have this bouquet! It's immeasurably more than you asked or thought!'"[97]

My circumstances have not changed. I still live in the same place, but I am comfortable knowing God's presence fills my home. My days are filled with pressures and deadlines, but God is with me. I'm still unclear about so many things, but God has the answers. Everything is still the same, except for one thing: It is the supernatural power of God that enables me to see my circumstances differently. What *has* changed is my heart!

Now I say with confidence, "I know that power! I know that strength!"

> "Now to Him who is able to do exceeding abundantly beyond all that we ask or think, according to the power that works within us; to Him be the glory in the church and in Christ Jesus to all generations forever and ever. Amen" (Ephesians 3:20 NASB).

– Chapter Twenty-Nine –

This Is Your Manassah!

Another year, another Christmas. I wanted it to be special. The joy I'd prayed for filled my heart. There was no other way to explain it. The church family where my husband and I had ministered had responsibly, thoughtfully, and lovingly cared for me. God had touched my life through friends!

Cards, rose buds, mowed lawns, flowers, pizzas—each brought a loving hug. Concerts, "let's-do-lunches," and a hilarious play in town delighted my soul. And the list continued!

A staff pastor, with more important things to do, came over to replace a burned out light bulb on my front porch. One of my neighbors kept my gutters clean. A door on the tool shed got a much needed paint job. Rides to the airport eased my load, and a precious stuffed rabbit reminded me of how good God was to comfort me with such friends. These friends were the "immeasurably more than I could ask or think" gifts from God!

So what can I do? I've got to do something! I've got to celebrate! Somehow I've got to let these people know how special they have been to me! But how?

An exciting idea popped into my mind. "What about a Christmas open house?" It grew greater, "WHAT ABOUT A CHRISTMAS OPEN HOUSE?" And finally it shouted! "WHAT ABOUT A CHRISTMAS OPEN HOUSE? "

"That's a *fantastic* idea," I said to myself. "I think I'll have a Christmas open house!"

I shared my enthusiasm with my counselor who had helped me keep focused on the power of God during this healing time. He politely waited until I was finished then asked, "Do you know what Joseph named his first son?"

"No."

"Joseph named his first born Manassah." He continued, "Do you know the literal Hebrew meaning for Manassah?" Again I had no idea. "Manassah means 'the sting is gone.' This open house will be your Manassah. God is removing the sting in your heart and replacing it with His joy."

I thought, "Joseph, the one who was hated by his brothers and sold into slavery. Joseph, who felt every pulse of his rejection. Joseph, who had desperately longed for his father and the love from his brothers. He named his son Manassah.

"Manassah. Why, every time he called his son, he was reminded of the reason for the name. Manassah! A good reason for an open house. God *is* removing the sting in my heart!"

With the help of a graphic designer, Psalm 28:6, 7 was beautifully inscribed on my invitation:

> "Blessed be the Lord, Because He has heard the voice of my supplications! The Lord is my strength and my shield; My heart trusted in Him, and I am helped; Therefore my heart greatly rejoices, And with my song I will praise Him."

Excitedly I began my preparations late one unseasonably warm November night. During the midnight hours I placed hundreds of tiny white lights in all the bushes in front of the house. Finishing around 2 A.M., I tested them before the cul-de-sac awakened. When I flipped the switch, I felt like the president lighting the national Christmas tree!

I decorated my whole house! Candles lit up every window and garlands hung from pillar to post. The Christmas tree twinkled, while luminaries brightened the driveway. Lights were everywhere. I didn't want my house to shine, I wanted it to dazzle! Make a statement! Astonish everyone!

After a few final touches, I took one last look at the table filled with beautifully arranged refreshments and savored the Christmas wassail brewing on the stove to be shared by friends. I threw open the door and hugged more than forty guests: my neighbors, bosses, co-workers and friends.

During this exciting evening I gathered everyone in the living room while I introduced them and shared how each had shown me his love and good works![98]

I will never forget that crisp December evening. It evolved into one of the most beautiful and memorable nights of my life. I had a wonderful time. God's name was exalted, and I was *thrilled* that I had done it!

> "Your love has given me great joy and encouragement, because you have refreshed the heart of 'this saint'" (Philemon 7).

– Chapter Thirty –

A Prayer for the Father of My Children

Never would I have believed that I would still be picking up pieces and working through the debris of my life from four years ago. "It's a lifetime process," a mother of five told me who had also felt the unspeakable sting of divorce. Through all the hurdles, hurts, and pain, God had done great things for me. He is still changing me from the inside out, and continues to burden me to pray for the one who walked away.

I called my *ex*-husband one Sunday afternoon to ask if he would be willing to meet me for lunch. His office was only a few miles from mine. This would be the first time in over three years that he and I had talked about something other than legal matters. There were still raw places in my heart that needed to heal, and I thought that a face-to-face encounter might help bring more closure. He agreed to meet.

Nervously, I leaned against one of the pillars outside my office building as I waited. After a somewhat awkward greeting, I suggested that we walk to a nearby carryout and pick up a couple of pitas. I had planned for us to eat on a park bench overlooking the Potomac River since it was a relatively mild March afternoon. But as soon as we were seated, dark clouds suddenly formed sending a cold pelting rain that forced us to retreat to a deli nearby.

Ignoring the people who were walking back and forth to select sodas from the dispenser next to our table, I focused on what I wanted to share: how God had sustained me through the most difficult time in my life. I also wanted the father of my children to know that I didn't hate him, nor did I regret knowing him, loving him, and sharing thirty years of my life with him.

After lunch as we stepped outside, I handed him this prayer that I'd recently written in my journal, hoping he might get a glimpse of what God was doing in my heart:

> Lord, what an absolutely gorgeous afternoon! As I sit out here on the deck, sipping coffee, and listening to the wind chimes play in the soft breeze, my face is warmed by a zillion sunbeams as I stretch from this winter's long nap!
>
> I wonder if there are others enjoying these same moments. Surely, I'm not the only one basking in Your warmth or enjoying the beauty of your brushstroke across the skies. I'm sharing Your goodness with those who know You and those who do not. You do not hold back Your faithfulness for a few. Your goodness can be enjoyed by all. The sun warms their faces just as much as it does mine.[99]
>
> Well, Lord, You've seen me through my fourth winter; and what a winter that was! Snow, freezing temperatures, ice—and more snow! The blizzard of '96 was history in the making. You wrapped Your arms around me and covered me with warm blankets of love and protection. You kept that old furnace going. What a miracle! Thank you again, Lord, for watching over me.

By the way, I've noticed that the path we've walked lately has been relatively smooth. No hurdles! No ruts! No stones! Unbelieveable!

Lord, remember those days when together we walked through that valley of the shadow of death? Sharp jagged rocks and treacherous pitfalls were everywhere. Haunting nightmares kept me awake. I felt as though I had been beaten thirty-nine times by one who held a metal-tipped whip, unable to move. Lord, that was so hard to bear!

But I also remember when You picked me up and held me in Your arms. Your words of comfort were a soothing ointment to my wounds.

Father, this is not what I wanted. How often I prayed that my marriage would have been the one that would break the chains that bound our parents' marriage failures. Lord, please guard my children's families. Don't allow another tragedy to touch the next generation. Please break the heart of the father of my children. May this not continue on.

This dad doesn't realize that if he would only be willing to seek You with his whole heart, then You would bring healing and wholeness not only to his life, but to the lives of those who were precious to him—lives which were once shattered, but, because of You, not hopelessly destroyed. He doesn't realize that he could gain far more respect from his children if he allowed You to change his heart rather than thinking that sooner or later everyone will have to "get over it," because he is just fine. That's straight from the pit of hell, isn't it, Lord? He is being deceived by Your enemy. He tries to hide, but Lord, he cannot hide from You!

I wish the father of my children knew how much his children longed for him to repent; they wonder how long he will choose to reject You.

I can't imagine how much he must hurt yearning to restore the relationship he once had with our children, in an environment of forgiveness, openness, and vulnerability.

I can't imagine how dark his nights must be and overcast are all his days. He is consumed by hours and hours of work, worn down, perhaps wondering at the end of a grueling day if he might discover, like Joseph's brothers, that a silver cup has been placed in his pouch of grain.[100] The detection would be frightening, Your consequences unknown, but done in love to bring about the gift of restoration—to bring about good.

I can't imagine how long he can go on without knowing You in a deep and intimate way. For I know that when You are first in his heart, then he will finally have peace and seek what is right.

Lord, thank You for Your faithfulness. I love it when I look to You and with a smile You shower me with Your blessings! Thank you for blessing me with friends—friends who are real, friends who still stand in the gap, friends whose hearts You burden to pray. How privileged is the father of my children to have them whisper his name before Your throne of grace. He doesn't understand how much Your people love him and want what is best for him. He will never know how much he was loved, and is still loved today.

Lord, I can never stop believing that one day the heart of this dad, for whom we continually pray, will come to You through the valley of brokenness. I can never stop believing that he will once again bring honor—not disgrace—to Your name. I pray that one day he will hear You say,

"Blessed are those whose lawless deeds have been forgiven, and whose sins have been covered."[101]

> Lord, it is getting a little dark. I can't see beyond that tree. I've enjoyed sitting out here with You so much, but it's time to go in. I wonder, where will we walk tomorrow? Will there be hills to climb, a wall to leap over, or a valley ahead? Will the day be pleasant like today, or will these winds that are picking up bring in a cold front? Oh, it really doesn't matter as long as You are here. I couldn't bear to go on without You. I just couldn't. And all these questions, all my concerns, I know I can't fix them, only You. I'm so thankful that I can give them all to You. Thank You, Lord, that you are always with me, no matter what!

As we stood outside the deli, my ex-husband tucked my unread prayer in his coat pockt. Departing he commented, "I'm glad you're okay."

Surprised by such a remark, I didn't know how to respond. "Okay?!" Was that similar to, 'Have a good day'?

I wanted to believe that he meant something more. I wanted to believe that "okay" meant he saw God's power radiating in my life, but I will never know. I'm not sure what prompted him, but he repeated a little more emphatically, "I *really* am glad you're okay."

With a million things I could have said, the only word that came out of my mouth was, "Amen!"

It was hard to shake his hand as if we were casual acquaintances. It was hard to realize that I would never feel his hug again. It was hard to believe we lived in different worlds. It was hard to turn and walk away.

– Epilogue –

I Have the Oil

Donna, there is going to be a 30-year anniversary celebration for the church. We will have it outside so the entire congregation can be together. As part of this occasion, the staff has planned for three people to share five-minute testimonies before the keynote speaker. We would like for you to be one of these people. Pray about it and let us know."

When I had first heard about this event, I wasn't sure why the leadership had decided to do it. So I had planned to go out of town to see my dad. Why would the church even plan an anniversary celebration? My husband had been on staff for eighteen of those thirty years.

But when I was asked to share a brief testimony, I knew! It was the same "I knew" when God had arranged my dinner invitation on one of those bleak weekends. It was the same, "I knew" when God prompted me to have a Christmas open house. It was the same, and I recognized it! God was working out an incredible plan! I didn't need to pray about it. I KNEW! The joy was already in my heart!

"Wow! Lord, I can't believe it! Look at what You've done in my heart!

I called Alan, the church administrator, to let him know.

"Yes, I'll do it! I'll praise His name!"

We laughed when Alan said, "If I had asked you to do this five years ago, you would have been under a chair!"

The staff and leadership had also been through some very hard times, as well. Many questions were discussed among them. What could they have done to prevent this, as a church? Were they to blame? Did they place too many unrealistic expectations on this pastor? In humility we had all knelt in prayer confessing our many shortcomings. As we arose from prayer, the Spirit of the Lord swept our doubts away. Why not have a celebration! Why not begin a new!

God had given me an opportunity like none other—to lift up His name before the whole congregation! I would also personally thank the body of Christ for lovingly caring and praying for me. Never once had I heard that I had been an embarrassment to them. Truly, they had been an extension of God's love. I wanted to let them know of the awesome miracle that had taken place in my life! I was "pumped," and God knew it!

The day finally came. It started out a little blustery—cool with a slight mist—which initially caused concern. But finally the sun broke through and a faint rainbow appeared for a brief time, then faded away. The temperature climbed as the excitement grew. It turned out to be an absolutely gorgeous fall day cooled by a soft breeze. A canopy of beautiful blue skies and large, billowy white clouds hovered over the congregation as if to participate in our worship. As I stepped up to the platform, I remembered a special admonition from a sermon by Dr. Stanley.

"Don't give up on God! Persevere! If you will keep on striving, fixing your eyes on Jesus, then one day you will see the bluest skies, the whitest, fluffiest clouds, and the brightest rainbows of your Christian walk. I guarantee it!"

I stood before the congregation knowing the Holy Spirit had prepared me for this moment. I looked beyond the skies, wanting to catch my Father's nod of approval. I envisioned Jesus, the Son of God, leaning over and whispering, "There's Donna, Father. She's one for whom I died! Let's listen as she shares with the people what our Spirit has laid on her heart!"

With my heart beating excitedly, I enthusiastically opened with these indelible words etched in my heart!

"There *is* a God! And God is *real*! There is power and strength in the Name of the Lord! My prayer today is that what I share with you will filter into the deafening ear. May the news penetrate the doubting hearts. I want to shout it from the mountain tops! So I will say it again! There is a God, and God is real! There is power and strength in the name of the Lord!

> 'For you, O God, have tested [me],
> You have refined [me] as silver is refined.
> You brought [me] into the net;
> You laid affliction on [my] back.
> You have caused men to ride over [my] head;
> [I] went through fire and through water;
> But You brought me out to rich fulfillment' (Psalm 66:10-12 NKJV).

"God picked up His daughter and set me before you today. This truly is a miracle! Those who have known me in the past now know that God has put a new song in my heart. He picked up the ashes of my life and covered me with His hands. He anointed me with oil and held me close to His heart. He then told me how much He loved me. He instructed me in His unfailing love. He taught me about forgiveness and poured out His blessings upon me.

"I praise His holy name! He is the One who lifted my head. He held my face in His hands and said, 'Donna, look at Me and nothing else. I am your Abba Father. I will catch the tears that fall and wipe them away.'

"Isaiah 1:4, 6 says, 'They have abandoned the Lord. They have despised the Holy One of Israel. They have turned away from Him.' Lord, I can't imagine how Your heart must have ached in pain. You were rejected by us all!

"'From the sole of the foot, even to the head, There is nothing sound in it. Only bruises, welts and raw wounds. Not pressed out or bandaged, nor softened with oil.' What a tragic picture of those who choose to live this way when there is a way out!

"The Lord is shouting from His Word, 'Can't you hear! Can't you see! I have the oil! I can soften, press out, and bandage the wounds!'

"His anger is not spent! But His hand is still stretched out. What a loving God I serve!

"Lord, thank You for allowing me to see that You will never stop reaching out. There is no end to Your love. There is no end to your comfort. Lord, there is no end to Your power to heal.

"David blessed the Lord in sight of all the assembly, and that's what I want to do today. So I share this moment with David! Taken from the book of I Chronicles 29:11-13, I say, "Move over David, because Donna is going to bless the Lord!'

"You, O Lord, it is You Who are great and powerful. Glory, victory, and majesty are Yours. Both riches and honor come from You. And in Your hand is power and might; it lies in Your hand to make great and to strengthen everyone. Now, God, I thank You and praise Your glorious name!

"Today I shout! Today I say with confidence! I *know* that power! I *know* that strength! Thank you for encouraging me! Thank you for praying for me!

"To God be the glory! He has done great things!"

– Endnotes –

1. II Corinthians 12:9
2. Romans 8:32
3. John 10:10b
4. Psalm 34:15a
5. I Chronicles 28:20
6. John 10:10b
7. Proverbs 3:5
8. Isaiah 54:5a
9. Matthew 6:8b
10. I Peter 5:7
11. Joshua 1:5
12. Psalm 139:17
13. Psalm 53:2
14. John 15:16
15. Luke 15:4; 19:10
16. John 3:16
17. Jeremiah 31:3
18. Deuteronomy 31:6b
19. Hebrews 13:5b
20. Psalm 100:5
21. Psalm 84:11b
22. Romans 8:37; Psalm 60:12
23. Psalm 145:14, 17, 18
24. Hannah, John D., "Grace and the Spiritual Life in John Owen," unpublished speech (1995).
25. Titus 3:4, 5a
26. Ephesians 2:4, 5
27. John 14:2
28. Revelation 19:9
29. Isaiah 58:9
30. Psalm 22:24
31. Philippians 4:7
32. Psalm 37:5
33. Isaiah 65:11
34. Deuteronomy 32:35a
35. Zephaniah 3:5
36. Psalm 111:7
37. Psalm 46:10
38. II Chronicles 16:9
39. James 1:17
40. Deuteronomy 31:6
41. II Corinthians 12:10
42. II Corinthians 2:15
43. John 3:16
44. Micah 6:8
45. Romans 5:8
46. Hebrews 12:1
47. I Timothy 1:5
48. Galatians 4:6
49. Philippians 3:14
50. James 4:7
51. Psalm 148:2; 103:20
52. Psalm 3:3
53. Matthew 8:26
54. Luke 8:25
55. James 5:16
56. Psalm 56:8
57. Hebrews 4:12
58. Hebrews 4:12
59. John 6:67
60. Proverbs 21:1
61. Malachi 2:16
62. Joshua 6:2
63. Acts 12:5
64. Acts 16:25
65. Isaiah 54:5
66. Revelation 19:6
67. Tozer, A.W., *The Pursuit of God* (Camp Hill, PA: Christian Publications, 1993) p.23.
68. II Corinthians 10:4 NIV
69. II Corinthians 11:3 NIV
70. II Corinthians 10:5 NIV
71. Lamentations 3:22, 23
72. John 10:10
73. II Corinthians 12:9
74. James 1:14
75. James 1:15
76. Hebrews 12:1
77. Tozer, A.W., *The Pursuit of God* (Camp Hill, PA: Christian Publications, 1993) pp.94-95
78. I Chronicles 22:5
79. I Kings 6:28
80. Exodus 26:1
81. Galatians 5:22
82. II Kings 4:5-7
83. Luke 22:31
84. Romans 8:16
85. Barnes, Craig M., *When God Interrupts* (InterVarsity Press, 1996) p.54.
86. Hebrews 12:2
87. John 6:66
88. Matthew 8:20
89. I Peter 1:8
90. Ephesians 3:20
91. Hebrews 10:22
92. Hebrews 4:16
93. Hebrews 10:19
94. I John 1:7
95. John 14:6
96. Philippians 3:13, 14
97. Ephesians 3:20b
98. Hebrews 10:24
99. Matthew 5:45
100. Genesis 44:2
101. Romans 4:7, 8

Lord, I Need a Hug
Order Form

Donna (Christensen) Bos
1016 Tribayne Ct.
Apex, NC 27502

(919) 355-2434

Please send *Lord, I Need a Hug* to:

Name: ______________________________________

Address: ____________________________________

City: ____________________ State: _______

Zip: _________

Telephone: (_____) _______________

Book Price: $10.00

Shipping: $3.00 for the first book and $1.00 for each additional book to cover shipping and handling within US, Canada, and Mexico. International orders add $6.00 for the first book and $2.00 for each additional book